Soaking
in God's Presence

Table of Contents

Introduction

Chapter 1	The Heart of Soaking	7
Chapter 2	Being Still	19
Chapter 3	Learning to Lean	33
Chapter 4	The Rhythm of Heaven	43
Chapter 5	Resting is Receiving	53
Chapter 6	Beholding is Becoming	65
Chapter 7	The Royal Priesthood	77
Chapter 8	Inquiring at His Temple	97
Chapter 9	Creating a Culture of Soaking	107

Introduction

Soaking prayer is not a new discovery as much as it is a recovery of a spiritual path to a lifestyle of intimacy with God paved by countless heroes of the faith. This type of prayer has been known in the past as waiting upon the Lord, being still, resting in the Lord, tarrying in His Presence, meditative and contemplative prayer.

A genuine Christian life is an impossible prospect without prayer. It is like getting married without ever connecting with your mate. Intimacy is only established through deep union and communication between individuals. In the same way in our relationship with God, there's no other way to know Him deeply apart from being with Him.

In the Bible and throughout history, we see countless men and women come into deep intimacy and knowledge of God in their face-to-face encounters with Him. From that place they came out empowered and transformed. They became the very agents of change to the world around them.

Jesus taught us how to pray, "Your kingdom come, Your will be done on earth as it is in heaven." God wants us to partner with Him in accomplishing His Will on this earth. Prayer is the starting point. However, it's important to know that there is much more to prayer than petition and asking for our needs to be met. At the core, prayer is coming to a place of deep union with God, our spirit with His Spirit, being filled with Him and coming out from that place bringing and releasing His supernatural world to the world around us.

There's more to soaking prayer than just being silent before God. As we soak deeper we experience the depths of His glory- His love, His goodness, and His power. This brings us to a deep knowledge and intimacy with God. In that place, we are transformed into His likeness, and transformed lives have the power to transform other lives.

Intimacy is a key to greater spiritual authority and power. We need to grow in intimacy to be able to enforce God's Will on earth "as it is in heaven" effectively. To the degree that His Presence and glory influence us, we will influence those around us. I find soaking prayer very effective on establishing a lifestyle of intimacy with God as an individual and in creating a culture that will host His presence corporately.

This manual will serve as a guide for you to develop a lifestyle of intimacy with God- seeing His face and hearing His voice, through soaking prayer. We hope to inspire you to develop and deepen your personal journey in the secret place with the Lord. There are several Scriptures and practical steps provided to aid you in this journey of discovering the depths of God through soaking prayer. The end of every chapter serves as a practical guide for you to discover and experience the different facets of soaking prayer.

CHAPTER 1

The Heart of Soaking

As we yearn for Him, He comes and makes Himself known to us His sons and daughters. Encounters with God bring our entire being – spirit, soul and body to a place of being saturated with His Presence.

In Pursuit of God

Psalm 63:1
O God, you are my God; I shall seek you earnestly; my soul thirsts for you; my flesh yearns for you, in a dry and weary land where there is no water.

David was a great forerunner of intimacy. He came to a place of favor with God because of his heart. No wonder he is known to be a man after God's own heart. He knew God intimately and he wrote of Him and his encounters with Him with such depth and passion that only a man of genuine experiences would be able to express. His journey with God will always be an inspiration to everyone. He knew God's heart, His ways and the facets of His Nature. He lived a life of relentless pursuit of God.

At one point, Saul was coming after him to kill him. Alone in the wilderness, he cried out, *"O God, you are my God; I shall seek you earnestly; my soul thirsts for you; my flesh yearns for you, in a dry and weary land where there is no water."* He went on to say, *"Your love is better than life."* He knew what *the priority* of his life was, it was to seek God, and it is far greater than securing his own life. In the midst of adverse situations and physical conditions he found himself in, he was unrelenting in his desire to gaze upon His beauty and inquire in His temple. Such was the heart of David, the man *after* God's own heart.

At a young age he learned to value His Presence more than anything else. When he became king, his passion for God never waned. In fact, in Psalm 108:1 he said, *"My heart is steadfast, O God; I will sing, I will sing praises, even with my soul."* Steadfast! Fixed! Immovable! That's the heart of David before God. Early on, during his reign, he established a tabernacle for the Lord because he desired to have a habitation for God and he would not settle for just intermittent visitations of Him. In fact, he instituted 24/7 nonstop praise and worship before God selecting the most skilled and anointed Levites to lead the rest of the people. His heart for God was so big that he wanted others to come into the same encounters he had with Him in the secret place.

Psalm 27:4 gives us a picture of the kind of devotion David lived out for God. He opened up a way for the rest of the nation of Israel to experience God in the place of intimacy. His personal lifestyle became a corporate blessing and an inspiration to all.

Psalm 27:4
One thing I have asked from the LORD, that I shall seek: That I may dwell in the house of the LORD all the days of my life, to behold the beauty of the LORD and to meditate in His temple.

Soaking Prayer

We live in a noise-polluted information age. In just one click of a button we can access the rest of the world through the worldwide web. Today, everything is fast, sleek, and we love it that way. Amidst development and progress, there are competing forces around us that demand our attention- from our favorite television programs, to latest movies, to video games, to sports, not to mention the demands of our jobs and domestic responsibilities. Being still is a big challenge. There will always be more things to do, deadlines to beat and pressures to face. At times the mere thought of these concerns derails us from the place of peace into a downward spiral of anxiety. If we could just hit the pause button and find our peace for a while, we wouldn't mind it at all.

The way we define something determines the way we approach it. From a religious standpoint, prayer is a duty to be performed to gain heaven's merits. But from a relationship view, it is a privilege to be treasured and sought after. Like any spiritual disciplines that we do, soaking prayer can be approached and applied either way. But the former reason is never God's intended reason for us to come near to Him.

What is soaking in the Presence of God? Soaking prayer is focusing all of our being - spirit, soul and body, to commune with God. It is a prayer of meditation and contemplation in which the unseen faculties (heart, mind and will, spirit) are in deep fellowship with God while the body is restful and the heart responds accordingly to the inner workings of the Spirit of God. It is gazing and looking intently to the Lord, our Father, with the spiritual eyes of our heart through our Truth-inspired, Spirit-guided imagination. It is devoting time to hear His voice and see His face, allowing Him to speak to us through visions, impressions, audible voice, and scriptures. It is staying in His Presence and allowing the Holy Spirit to fill us with more of Him.

In soaking, everything in us hungers for Him. A deep longing and anticipation to know the facets of His nature rise within. As we yearn for Him, He comes and makes Himself known to us His sons and daughters. Encounters with God bring our entire being - spirit, soul and body to a place of being saturated with His Presence. Think of a dry sponge. Imagine it being dipped slowly in a pail of water. Over time, it will soak up all the water that it can. I would like to think that this is what exactly David did in the Presence of God; he soaked and waited upon the Lord with all of his heart. In soaking, everything in us is inundated with His Presence.

It's all about Love

Matthew 3:16-17
After being baptized, Jesus came up immediately from the water; and behold, the heavens were opened, and he saw the Spirit of God descending as a dove and lighting on Him, and behold, a voice out of the heavens said, "This is My beloved Son, in whom I am well-pleased."

Jesus began His ministry knowing that His Father loves Him and is proud of Him even before He started doing miracles and healings because He is the Beloved Son of God. Everything about Jesus is about the Father. Everything He did is motivated by the Father's love. Jesus was able to do the things He did because He knew the Father's heart and He is acquainted with all of His ways.

John 5:18-20
For this reason therefore the Jews were seeking all the more to kill Him, because He not only was breaking the Sabbath, but also was calling God His own Father, making Himself equal with God. Therefore Jesus answered and was saying to them, "Truly, truly, I say to you, the Son can do nothing of Himself, unless it is something He sees the Father doing; for whatever the Father does, these things the Son also does in like manner. For the Father loves the Son, and shows Him all things that He Himself is doing; and the Father will show Him greater works than these, so that you will marvel.

Every individual has a driving force within. It could be a goal or a desire for power, money, status or position. What about Jesus, what do you think was the driving force behind all that He did amidst the persecutions, unbelief and evil? It was the love of the Father. The passion of Jesus, more than anything, is the Father and everything that's about Him. He lived to please Him. Love was the motivation for everything that He did. This love strengthened and empowered Him from within allowing Him to face every challenge and persecution with such assurance and confidence. It is this love that enabled Him to release forgiveness to the worst of sinners, and became the author of salvation through His death on the cross.

Like Jesus, there could be no greater motivation in all that we do for God but love. Knowing that the Father loves us completely and we are accepted in Him 100% *is* the driving force to know Him even more and be with Him constantly. He is the kindest person we could ever be with. He is the highest, the greatest, the Almighty, yet He is the nearest to us and He loves us completely because He is our Father.

Like Jesus, there could be no greater motivation in all that we do for God but love.

What spurs you to pray or to stay a little bit longer in His Presence? If it's to try to do well, or perform harder to earn "points" of favor, then you will miss the point. Performance or religion will choke the life out of our times with God. In everything that we do, may this be the core motivation— *my Father loves me and I love Him.* The devil may come to intimidate and tempt us or undermine our authority as God's children. But we will remain under God's authority because we are His sons and daughters and that He loves us. All schemes of the enemy are automatically out of the picture whenever we remain in the love of the Father. Jesus overcame every single obstacle He faced with love.

Love, not the law, compels us to know Him deeper. Our hearts respond to the love that He gives. The more we taste of His goodness and nearness the deeper we desire to be with Him. Remember, we have been created to be intimate with our Father. By the Holy Spirit, we have the access and the ability to know Him deeper. Our job is to *be loved* because we are His *beloved* sons and daughters.

Be Overwhelmed

God loves us. In the Old Testament, that love was evident. In Psalm 8, we see David being overwhelmed by the greatness and majesty of God. He talked of His marvelous heavens and how He set the stars in their rightful places. Moreover, he was just as amazed to know that God cares for mankind, that He crowned them with glory and honor and put them in the place of dominion above all things. This particular psalm gives us a glimpse of one of the secrets of David- which was meditating upon the Lord and allowing His bigness to overwhelm him.

Psalm 8:3-6
When I consider Your heavens, the work of Your fingers, the moon and the stars, which You have ordained; what is man that You take thought of him, and the son of man that You care for him? Yet You have made him a little lower than God, and You crown him with glory and majesty! You make him to rule over the works of Your hands; You have put all things under his feet.

To be overwhelmed by God is the core experience in soaking. As we gaze upon His majesty and beauty, we are overwhelmed with His greatness and His goodness. In that place, all the noise and concerns around us, fades. The moment

The moment He comes to reveal Himself more, He lifts the veil of our spiritual eyes and we see clearly who He is to us and who we are in Him. Oh what a joy to be in the Presence of God!

He comes to reveal Himself more, He lifts the veil of our spiritual eyes and we see clearly who He is to us and who we are in Him. Oh what a joy to be in the Presence of God!

The Goal of Soaking Prayer

Exodus 33:11
Thus the LORD used to speak to Moses face to face, just as a man speaks to his friend When Moses returned to the camp, his servant Joshua, the son of Nun, a young man, would not depart from the tent.

Why didn't Joshua leave the Tent of Meeting with Moses? I would like to believe that he actually got soaked with the Presence of God and he loved it. By watching Moses, he had seen what intimacy with God could do to a man. I believe his desire went deeper than just to have his face shine like Moses'. He had tasted the sweetness of His presence, His glory, His nearness and he couldn't get enough of Him. And so he stayed a little bit longer. He loved His Presence and wanted more of Him. This is what compelled him to stay in the Presence of God.

Psalm 27: 8
When You said, "Seek My face," my heart said to You, "Your face, O LORD, I shall seek."

The goal of soaking prayer is communion and intimacy. It is coming to God face to face. The focus is God and not self. We come for God Himself, and not to ask for the answers to our needs. Intimacy necessitates deep communion and communion requires sharing of intimate thoughts and feelings. Developing intimacy with God warrants time. It takes time to go deep. Communion is taking the time to search His heart and allowing our hearts to be yielded and open to His inner workings. As we align our hearts to His, we hear His voice and experience Him deeper.

Jesus calls us His friends. More than obedience, ultimately, it is relationship that He desires from us. When we gaze upon Him, we see the face of a Friend. In intimacy, He reveals to us His secrets and He gives us keys of the Kingdom of God. As we read through the Bible we begin to see nuggets of wisdom and revelation as if suddenly we have been given a new set of glasses. We can read the same passage again and again and new things are still being revealed. This is because our Friend lifts the veil and reveals to us His marvelous secrets.

More than obedience, ultimately, it is relationship that He desires from us. When we gaze upon Him, we see the face of a Friend.

Questions for Personal Ponder or Group Discussion

1. Do you have the revelation of how much Father-God really loves you? If so, when did you receive that revelation?

2. What lifestyle changes do you need to make to ensure your relationship with God is being nourished through soaking prayer?

3. Are there distractions keeping you from being completely overwhelmed by God? What steps are you going to take towards removing them?

4. What are your goals for soaking prayer? Is it to strengthen your relationship with God? Deeper intimacy?

5. Are you ready to journey into a deeper communion with Father-God? To have the veil lifted, and to see clearly who He is?

Activation

Meditate on the fathering love of God using the Scriptures mentioned in this chapter. Let them inspire you to gaze upon His beauty and majesty. Ask the Father to develop in you the heart of intimacy.

Gleanings in His Presence

_____
_____
_____
_____
_____
_____
_____
_____
_____
_____
_____
_____
_____
_____
_____
_____
_____
_____

CHAPTER 2

Being Still

*Stillness and rest position our hearts to receive.
It is hard to receive from Him when we are striving.*

Be Still

Psalm 46:10
"Cease striving and know that I am God; I will be exalted among the nations, I will be exalted in the earth."

Soaking prayer is being still in the Presence of God. Although the body is at rest, the heart longs and yearns for the Lord. Soaking prayer is far from being passive. It is a dynamic thing to wait on Him with great expectancy within. We may be sitting comfortably or lying down, but our heart is wide open, sensitive to the leading of the Spirit, ready to receive from the Father. The heart is a container before God. The deeper we long *for* Him the more we receive *of* Him. Let yours be an empty vessel ready to be filled with His fullness.

Soaking prayer is far from being passive. In fact it is a dynamic thing to wait on Him with great expectancy within.

How do we soak? Finding a place that is set up to be conducive and offers some kind of privacy and silence is the first, practical starting point. It could be a particular area in your house, your office or your living room free from distractions. You can have soft music playing in the background. This could help a lot in getting you into the flow and focusing on Him. However, there are some people who would prefer complete silence. Choose what works best for you.

There are practical steps that we can follow when soaking. Whether alone or with a group, the following steps are valuable:

1. Quiet down
Psalm 62:5
My soul, wait in silence for God only, for my hope is from Him.

Next after finding a comfortable and quiet place to be alone with God is to quiet down your heart and your mind. This is not emptying your mind but filling it with longings and desires for God. This could be challenging for many, especially when the mind is used to working in hyper drive, having just gone through the grocery lists or suddenly remembering the car is low in oil, etc. The best way for me to focus and quiet down is to express my need and longing for Him. Sometimes I whisper a prayer, *"Oh Father I miss You, I thirst for You..."* As I go deeper in my longings, I sense the Spirit of God taking over my thoughts and guiding me deeper into His Presence.

Quieting our hearts may not come automatically, especially if we're not used to it. At the start it could be quite challenging. But like the way we develop our physical muscles, our spiritual muscles need constant exercise. Doing this again and again makes it easier.

2. Focus
Psalm 27: 4
One thing I have asked from the LORD, that I shall seek: that I may dwell in the house of the LORD all the days of my life, to behold the beauty of the LORD and to meditate in his temple.

Beauty in this verse means God's delightfulness – His goodness. By the Holy Spirit, we gaze at the beauty (delightfulness) of the Father. This is an important point; it is hard to set our eyes on an angry face. Whenever we come to Him we see His face shining with joy and love towards us. To gaze is to look intently and steadily. Remembering His loving kindness helps us focus on His nearness. We become aware of His desire to be with us, His children.

Let your heart understand that He delights in you, and He is filled with joy and anticipation to be with you. As you look intently in one facet of His character, for example goodness, He comes and saturates your whole being with a clear sense and awareness that He indeed is good. Then you come to a state in which you could really, really say you have tasted and have seen He is immeasurably good to you. Goodness becomes alive inside of you then. This experience is far deeper than any sermon or mere study of the Bible could afford. This is what revelation is all about.

What you focus on will be magnified within you. Like David seeing the universe, the stars and the moon, in one of his meditations (Psalm 8), he came to realize the greatness of God, His glory and His majesty. At that very moment he came to a clear understanding of man's value before the eyes of God. The Almighty God has crowned him with glory and majesty and He made him to be the ruler of His creation. David did not receive this revelation not by mere study or scientific observation of God's universe, he experienced God's Presence and character displayed in His works and he was left amazed.

Let your heart understand that He delights in you and that He is filled with joy and anticipation to be with you.

Focusing on the Lord also means to have an expectant heart for Him to come, much like a watchman waiting for the breaking of dawn. We focus our whole being with a deep sense of anticipation and excitement. We pay close attention in our spirit for whatever God has for us. The moment God shows up, we are ready to plunge into His Presence and not let go of Him.

To focus on Him is to be sensitive to the leading of the Holy Spirit. There will be times you will sense that your emotions, desires, joy and peace are being awakened as you allow Him to guide you deeper into the Presence of God. All these are the inner workings of the Holy Spirit. His Word becomes a living experience to us.

3. Longing and seeking
Psalm 84:1-2
How lovely are Your dwelling places, O LORD of hosts! My soul longed and even yearned for the courts of the LORD; My heart and my flesh sing for joy to the living God.

Deep calls unto deep, the psalmist wrote. Our hearts have the capacity to go deeper in desiring His Presence. David likened his yearning for God to a desert longing for water; let our hearts also desire God. The deeper we go in our desires and longings, the deeper He goes inside of us. The Spirit of God is our Teacher. He is the *'paraclete'*, the one Who walks alongside us. He will lead us deeper in the realms of the Father's Presence as we allow our hearts to be passionate in pursuing Him.

4. Respond to God
Psalm 34:8
O taste and see that the LORD is good; how blessed is the man who takes refuge in Him!

God's Presence comes in waves. Be sensitive to the flow of the Holy Spirit within you. Watch out for impressions rising within your heart as the Spirit of God leads you deeper. What I like about soaking is this: it is never boring. It is unpredictable yet exciting, to say the least. It is a journey. As our hearts and our thoughts focus on Him, our whole being responds to Him– our emotions, desires, creativity, passion, faith and dreams are awakened. Joy, peace, and love also fill our hearts.

As you go deeper in His Presence the Lord also reveals His heart to you. The Lord comes to us in different measures, tones and modes. He may come in a quiet whisper. Or He will paint a picture in your mind that would startle you or trigger thoughts and emotions that would release joy unspeakable. At other times you will see His face, or the heavenly realms, or angels. Sometimes He overwhelms you with His love flowing like a liquid fire into our being consuming fears, doubts, limitations, rejections, shame, and making you free. There will be times you will feel deep peace, or His glory comes like a weighty substance that covers your entire body. Your faculties become so sensitive in His Presence. It is true; you are more alive in His Presence.

In His Presence

Psalm 46:10
"Cease striving and know that I am God; I will be exalted among the nations, I will be exalted in the earth."

Soaking positions us in stillness and rest. Our Father invites us to be still in His Presence and to know He is God. In that place He reveals new facets of His Nature. What is revealed to us becomes part of us. The revelation of His Fathering Love for example does something deep to the core of our being. Suddenly we see and understand clearly that we are His sons indeed. It's more than just information, it is a revelation that results to inner conviction and assurance.

Stillness and rest position our hearts to receive. It is hard to receive from Him when we are striving. Many times when He speaks to us, He speaks in whispers, in still, small voice. This necessitates undivided attention and a restful spirit. It is in hearing that we receive from Him.

Everything in the kingdom is not to be achieved, but received. We best receive in the place of rest. Romans 14: 17 states *that the kingdom of God is righteousness, peace, and joy in the Holy Spirit.* We must be in the Holy Spirit and remain in peace and rest to be able to align our whole being with heaven. When we are at rest, God can do the rest. When we cease striving, He is able to reveal and impart more to us.

Heart Matters

2 Chronicles 16:9a
For the eyes of the LORD move to and fro throughout the earth that He may strongly support those whose heart is completely His.

We were designed to be filled with and to contain His Manifest Presence. The state of our hearts before God is of utmost importance because all Kingdom matters are matters of the heart. The heart is the gateway to different realms, physical or spiritual. If our heart is focused on the physical realm, we will be limited to what our senses would dictate. However if our heart is focused on God, the spiritual realm becomes our reality.

All Kingdom matters are matters of the heart.

The moment God released His breath - *ruach* - to Adam, he stood up as a living being. Every cell, every fiber of Adam, spirit, soul and body was created to host, to contain, to be filled with the Presence of God. Nothing has changed in Christ; everything has been restored.

We are given the same privilege and experience Adam had before the Fall. God is seeking those hearts that are totally His so he can show Himself strong. The heart set toward heaven is attractive to Him. It is like a magnet for the blessings in the heavenly realms. We are children of the Kingdom and we are wired to be in His Presence.

Psalm 63:1
O God, You are my God; I shall seek You earnestly; my soul thirsts for You, my flesh yearns for You, in a dry and weary land where there is no water.

Psalm 63, which David wrote, gives us a closer look into his heart. As we meditate on this beautiful psalm, we can become overwhelmed with the first two words, *"O God!"* Why did David have to put the word *O* before God? Why not just say, *God, You are my God*? As we get into the spirit of the word, we can see a pure heart that's passionately longing and thirsting for God! The rest of the words in this psalm find their significance and weight from this first word. It revealed the depths of the heart of the one who is given the title, the man after God's own heart. It is always amazing to understand how the Sovereign God would allow Himself to be apprehended by our deep desires.

Soaking in the Word

There are different ways to soak in His Presence. Several excellent materials on soaking are available these days, including anointed songs and music, devotional materials, etc. We may listen to worship songs and rest in His presence. Another way is to soak in the Word. This is to meditate upon Him by reading through the words and narratives in the Scriptures and allowing the Holy Spirit to illuminate insights and revelations in our hearts. It is not a frantic reading, jumping from page to page because you don't understand a particular passage. It is reading at a pace that would enable you to ruminate or chew on every word as the Holy Spirit guides you. I find meditating upon the Word a crucial spiritual exercise in knowing Him deeper. His Word under the guidance of the Holy Spirit becomes the very entrance to deeper encounters with His Nature.

In His realm, His words are reality. When we meditate on His words, the reality of heaven comes down to us. As we soak with the right heart, His words become seeds sown in our hearts. As we choose to remain in His presence, the seeds will surely yield a great harvest - thirty, sixty and hundredfold.

We have to understand that God's words are settled in heaven but not yet completely established on earth. He looks for men whose hearts are ready to receive His words. We are to agree with Him the moment we receive His words and then declare it back to Him in prayer. In soaking, He gives us dreams and promises deep within our spirits. And under the influence and the power of the Holy Spirit we start to declare things into reality. His words from His world, burning in our hearts by the power of the Holy Spirit, become reality on this earth by our declaration. This is how we partner with heaven. This is how we release heavens reality here on earth.

Psalm 84:1
How lovely is your dwelling place, O LORD Almighty! (NIV)

By the guidance of the Holy Spirit, imagine, feel or sense what the authors are saying, or what the circumstances around them were as they wrote. Let your heart feel what they felt and long for Him the way they longed for Him. Sense their hearts and their passion in the psalm. Can you imagine what they were seeing and experiencing as they were standing before the glory of God? You can make this psalm your own prayer and be able to come into the same depths in the spirit like them.

Psalm 84:2
My soul yearns, even faints, for the courts of the LORD; my heart and my flesh cry out for the living God. (NIV)

Can you feel the longing of their hearts in these words? Soaking in the word necessitates our inward being to be engaged with the very heart and intents revealed through the words we read. Let your heart be yielded and learn to tap into the very heart of the Father. You will be amazed where the Holy Spirit leads you by the His Word. A regular or casual reading of the Word rarely gives us such depths of experience with God.

When the sons of Korah wrote Psalm 84, they were under the inspiration of the Holy Spirit and so those words are anointed. As we meditate on it by the Holy Spirit, we get to experience the flow of the same anointing. This is true throughout the rest of the books of the Bible because the Holy Spirit is the Author of God's Word aiding men to write words breathed in and inspired by Him.

Reading the Scriptures after soaking will yield a hundredfold of revelations. As you soak deep in the Presence of God, your heart becomes fertile and ready to receive the seeds of His revelations. You experience the life in the Word when you feed yourself with fresh manna. A message born in the head will reach only the head, but a message born in the heart will reach the heart because deep calls unto deep.

We are blessed so we can be channels of blessings to others. The more we receive from Him, the more we increase in capacity to give to others. An increase in revelation will have corresponding increase in our faith. Your mind is renewed, the Words become alive and life-giving, not just to you but to those who listen and receive the words you speak, the very words that came from your encounters with God in the secret place. As you know Him, you are being entrusted with more of Him.

Questions for Personal Ponder or Group Discussion

1. Where is your quiet place? Pick a physical location where you can enter into His presence without disturbance or distraction.

2. How committed are you to soaking? What steps can you take toward increasing your commitment?

3. Do you have specific bible verses or songs that help you quiet down? If not, start discovering what verses and/or songs help your heart and mind to quiet down and relax.

4. What facets or characteristics of God will you focus on when you begin soaking?

5. Which realm is your heart positioned toward, the physical or spiritual? Begin to focus your heart toward Father God and allow the spiritual realm to become a reality.

Activation

Psalm 46:10
" Be still, and know that I am God. I will be exalted among the nations, I will be exalted in the earth!" (NIV)

Let us remember that in stillness, God reveals Himself. Following the practical steps mentioned above, ask the Holy Spirit to guide you deeper into His Presence. You can use God's Word to guide you in your meditation.

Gleanings in His Presence

___
___
___
___
___
___
___
___
___
___
___
___
___

CHAPTER 3

Learning to Lean

As we learn to lean into the heart of God, we will be in sync with the rhythm of heaven.

- **Lean:**

verb -
1. To bend or slant away from the vertical.
2. To incline the weight of the body so as to be supported, slant.
3. To rely for assistance or support: have confidence or faith in.
4. To have a tendency or preference.
5. To set or place so as to be resting or supported.
6. To cause to incline.

noun - A tilt or an inclination away from the vertical.

Leaning back, as in a recliner, on a pillow, or a staff (Jacob in Hebrews 11:21) is an act of rest, relaxation, support. When you lean back on something or someone there is NO effort, just trust, security, peace, comfort, support, and out of that rest you gain new strength to rise up for the assignment.

Song of Solomon 8:5
Who is this coming up from the wilderness, leaning on her beloved?

This question is not being asked by the Bride or Bridegroom, but by the choir. As we lean on our lover, our Heavenly Father, and we come out of our time in the wilderness of being with Him, others will witness and experience the results of our leaning on Him, our relationship with Him, the peace, the security, support, and the power. Leaning on our Beloved, by faith; not leaning to our own understanding, nor trusting in any righteousness of our own; but in the strength of Him.

This scripture is also a reflection of Jesus' time in the wilderness with God. He leaned into the heart of His Father, and just like the Bride in Song of Solomon, came out of the wilderness ready for ministry and ushering in the Kingdom of God.

Throughout Jesus' three years of ministry, because of His time in the wilderness, He learned when to lean forward and when to lean back and was completely ready for His Assignment. Leaning forward is our assignment in ministry, etc., while leaning back is positioning ourselves in alignment in order to receive the downloads to fulfill our assignment. This is the rhythm of heaven.

II Samuel 3:1
Now there was a long war between the house of Saul and the house of David; and David grew steadily stronger, but the house of Saul grew weaker continually.

There is a great principle found in this scripture. When we learn how to lean back in the wilderness, we will become stronger in our leaning forward in the palace. Our wilderness times will produce our strongest times. We MUST cultivate a lifestyle of resting in the WILDERNESS, alignment, in order to dwell in the PALACE (a place of royalty and authority), and fulfill our assignment.

We must cultivate a lifestyle of resting in the wilderness.

Moses learned how to lean during his time in the wilderness which prepared him for his assignment, something he could not learn in the palace. Esther, Joseph and David learned how to lean during their wilderness dwellings which prepared them for their assignments, which led them into significant positions in the palace (Kingdom). God has a destiny for each of us and He knows what our individual wilderness experiences will produce for each of us.

There is a correlation between our wilderness dwellings and experiences, leaning back to experience the goodness and glory of God, and preparing us for leaning forward, demonstrating the Kingdom of God through love, power, and signs and wonders. Leaning back is ministering from His presence, while leaning forward is ministering from His authority.

A love relationship develops in our wilderness times. In Song of Solomon 8:5 Jesus is referred to as "Beloved", but in Deuteronomy 33:12 we are called "Beloved". The wilderness will cause hearts to lean into one another and will come to experience and understand the goodness of God in order to demonstrate the Kingdom of God. The disciple John is referred to as beloved. In Matthew 17:5 on the Mount of Transfiguration God declares, "This is my beloved Son, in whom I am well pleased." This is the second time the Father affirms His beloved son. Jesus wasn't just God's son, He was His beloved Son. There was a leaning of hearts together between Father and Son.

Deuteronomy 33:12
May the beloved of the Lord dwell in security by Him, Who shields him all the day and he dwells between His shoulders.

In this verse, Moses is at the end of his assignment and he is administering blessings to the twelve tribes of Israel. Moses decrees the blessing for the tribe of Benjamin to be to live on the chest of God. In other words, this tribe received the blessing to lean straight into the heart of God, hearing and feeling His heartbeat, His very breath on their foreheads in security, rest and comfort. Oh what a place to dwell. This is the SECRET place of the Most High, not a mountain or the cleft of the rock.

John 13:23
There was reclining on Jesus' breast one of His disciples, who Jesus loved. Peter, turning around saw the disciple whom Jesus loved (beloved) following them; the one who also had leaned back on His breast at the supper...

Jesus was also reclining at the table (John 13:21, Luke 22:14). John was leaning into the heart of Jesus as Jesus leaned into the heart of His Father. Jesus was approaching the most intense portion of His overall assignment - Gethsemane, his trial, and crucifixion. Because Jesus had learned how to lean into the heart of His Father, He only did what He saw the Father doing and only said what He heard His Father speaking. This principle was more important in His upcoming final days on earth than His former, and this only came by leaning into His Father's heart.

Jesus could release His heart, revelation, and secrets to John. Their hearts were connected. Peter argued with Jesus John had learned how to lean into the heart of Jesus, so when Jesus tried to wash his feet. When Jesus mentioned that one of them would betray him, they all began looking around at each other. Then Peter looked to John and asked him who it was Jesus was talking about and then John asked Jesus who it was. John had obtained a place of trust and closeness with Jesus because he learned how to lean into the heart of Jesus.

John had learned how to lean into the heart of Jesus.

John 13:21-26
When Jesus had said this, He became troubled in spirit and testified, and said, "Truly, truly I say to you that one of you will betray Me." The disciples began looking at one another, at a loss to know of which one He was speaking. There was reclining on Jesus' breast one of His disciples, whom Jesus love. Simon Peter therefore gestured to him and said to him, "Tell us who it is of whom He is speaking." He, leaning back thus on Jesus' breast, said to Him, "Lord, who is it?" Jesus therefore answered, "That is the one for who I shall dip the morsel and give it to him."

It was Jesus' desire to have all of His disciples (sons) to lean into His heart, but John is the only one, after three years, that "caught" it. John knew how to lean into the heart of Jesus. Jesus had John's heart and this is why he was denoted "as the one Jesus loved." The truth is, any one of the disciples could have had the same position John had with Jesus, and any one of them could have leaned into the breast of Jesus at the supper, but only John positioned himself for it. John was the first disciple to be with Jesus and he was the last disciple to remain because he quickly learned how to lean, he stepped directly into his alignment. And even in the Book of Revelation John is still leaning into the Father's heart receiving some of the greatest revelation ever given to man. John learned, just like Jesus, how to lean back and receive so he could lean forward and release. This is alignment for the assignment: supernatural kingdom revelation. John caught it immediately from the very beginning.

The setting at the Last Supper is similar to the setting with Elijah and Elisha. Elijah learned how to lean in the wilderness (I Kings 19:4) in order to complete his assignment. As the fifty prophets watched the relationship of Elijah and Elisha (II Kings 2:7), the eleven disciples watched the relationship of Jesus and John from a distance. We hope the prophets eventually "caught it". Even though it took the disciples a little more time to "catch it", they eventually did, but not till after Jesus had gone through the most excruciating moments on earth. When He needed them most, none stuck with him except John. John was there all the way to the cross. Though in scripture we're never given any indication Jesus was "a father" to John, He was God in the flesh and He represented Father God here on earth, and thus when our fathers go through excruciating, moments whether great or small, sons and daughters who have developed leaning into each other's hearts will stick with the fathers through it all.

Questions for Personal Ponder or Group Discussion

1. Have you learned how to put all assignments aside and just lean into Father God?

2. Have you learned how to take your wilderness (leaning) experiences and use them to fulfill your assignment?

3. What has your perception of "A wilderness experience" been in the past? Do you need to change your perception, and how?

4. Does Jesus have all of your heart so He can release His secrets to you? Why or why not?

5. What do you do when facing intense times of testings and trial?

Activation

Psalm 46:10
Be still, and know that I am God. I will be exalted among the nations; I will be exalted in the earth! (NIV)

Let us remember it is in stillness God reveals Himself. Following the practical steps mentioned above, ask the Holy Spirit to guide you deeper into His presence. You can use God's Word to guide you in meditation.

Gleanings in His Presence

_____
_____
_____
_____
_____
_____
_____
_____
_____
_____
_____
_____
_____
_____

CHAPTER 4

The Rhythm of Heaven

There are seasons of heaven where God will hide us, and others where He will reveal us.

Rhythm can be Compared to the Waltz

Holy Spirit is the best teacher to teach us the seasons of heaven. The rhythm is in the Holy Spirit, hearing the heartbeat of the Father. It is extremely necessary we are synced with the rhythm of heaven.

Jesus didn't think it odd to describe the culture of Heaven in terms of a dance. Neither did C. S. Lewis. In his book, Letters to Malcolm: Chiefly on Prayer, he wrote this about the unfettered joys of Heaven:

Dance and game are frivolous, unimportant, down here: for "down here" is not their natural place. Here, they are a moment's rest from the life we were placed here to live. But in this world everything is upside down. That which, if it could be prolonged here, would be a truancy, is likest that which in a better country is the End of ends. Joy is the serious business of heaven.

Joy is a serious business of heaven.

Joy is the serious business of heaven. What better way to express joy than by dancing, moving with the rhythm of heaven? The idea captivated me. I wasn't a dancer, let alone, a 'waltzer'. So I began researching the waltz and listening to waltzes to try to understand what He meant.

The term "waltz," I learned, is from the German word *walzen*, meaning "to roll, turn, or to glide." Originally a lively, joyful, country dance of the peasants in outlying areas of Vienna and in alpine regions of Austria, it is a simple dance, easily learned. It is characterized by two partners intertwining their arms at shoulder level, often touching cheek-to-cheek, and moving as one in 3/4 time (rhythm) with strong accent on the first beat and a basic pattern of step-step-close.

After a lot of thought, study, and prayer, I finally understood what the Holy Spirit revealed to me. The analogy that most accurately represents the rhythm of heaven is the image of the waltz. There is love in the waltz-partners delighting not only in the dance but in each other's company, holding each other, gazing into each other's eyes, whispering into each other's ears. There is joy in the waltz-a lively, breathless, exhilarating sense of being swept away. Finally, there is unity in the waltz-two partners moving as one, in step not only with the music but with each other.

Leif's Revelation of the Rhythm of Heaven

This all began for me one fall morning as I was ministering in a church in the Northeast. We had a couple of days of conference meetings and I stayed over to minister on Sunday morning. I had preached the first service and was now called to the platform to preach in the second service. When I approached the podium, the pastor asked everyone to stand up, put their hands out towards me and join him as he prayed a blessing over me. Just then the Spirit of God came upon me and I was on the floor totally overcome by the weightiness of His presence.

It was obvious to the pastor I was not getting up anytime soon. I knew God was telling me to just be still (soak) and wait on Him. Neither the pastor nor the congregation was use to anything quite like this. Not knowing what to do, the pastor called my personal assistant up to take the microphone. As my personal assistant shared for about 20 minutes, God began to teach me about the rhythm of heaven.

He began to reveal to me there's a time to lean back (receive) and lean forward (re-lease). Interestingly enough, my personal assistant was experiencing this truth, as well. As I was leaning back, my personal assistant was leaning forward. We were moving with the rhythm of heaven, and it was at this time God began to download to me the revelation of the waltz and how it compared to the rhythm of heaven.

The result of this beautiful rhythm was God moved in that service in a very powerful and transforming way. After I had been leaning back for about twenty minutes receiving, the Lord released me to get up, lean forward and release. However before I stood up, the pastor tried to help me up and as I put my hand out to him, the power of God came upon him and he fell down under the Spirit. Next his wife came and the same happened to her. Then one person after another came up to me and the power of God would hit them and they would go down. I believe God was trying to teach this precious pastor and his congregation about leaning back to receive and being still to KNOW Him.

As I stood to my feet, God gave me very clear instructions. He wanted us to do the waltz. Yes, you read that right, the waltz. By this time the platform and the altar was flooded with people wanting a touch from God. I began to pronounce the waltz, "Da-da-da-da-da...da da, da da... Da-da-da-da-da...da da, da da... Da-da-da-da-da...da da, da da... Da-da-da-da-da...da da, da da...", and so on. This went on for over one and a half hours; over and over we pronounced the waltz. As I did this I blessed close to one thousand people. Hundreds of people were powerfully ministered to that morning. Some went through deliverance, while others melted in God's love and wept like babies, and others were drastically saved. The rhythm of heaven spilled out into the sanctuary...into the foyer...and out to the parking lot. I can be honest with you and say that church has never been the same since.

We must move with the rhythm of heaven.

We have experienced the waltz in other settings since that service and God has always moved in very powerful ways. Now I'm not suggesting we make a doctrine out of this. If my flesh I would have tried this without leaning back and receiving, it would have probably been a total disaster and I would have never been invited back to minister in that church again. The point God was wanting to make clear is we must move with the rhythm of heaven....to know what He's doing and when to do it.

Exodus 24:15 & 16
Then Moses went up to the mountain, and the cloud covered the mountain. The glory of the LORD rested on Mount Sinai, and the cloud covered it for six days; and on the seventh day He called to Moses from the midst of the cloud.

Genesis 1:31 - 2:2
God saw all that He had made, and behold, it was very good. And there was evening and there was morning, the sixth day. Thus the heavens and the earth were completed, and all their hosts. By the seventh day God completed His work which He had done, and He rested on the seventh day from all His work which He had done.

These two specific scriptures truly demonstrate the rhythm of heaven. In Exodus 24, Moses and Joshua are on Mount Sinai leaning back, resting, soaking...as the Lord Himself rested on the mountain. This went on for six days. Then on the seventh day He spoke! In Genesis 1 God leans forward and releases for six days and then on the seventh day he leans back and rests. We also must learn the rhythm of heaven... when to lean back and receive, and when to lean forward and release.

Genesis 1:26
Let Us make man in Our image, according to Our likeness. (emphasis added)

God said let us make a partnership that looks like us, loves like us, dances like us. Let us extend our family. Let us expand the culture of Heaven in an ever-widening circle that will begin with two people (you and Him), and fill the earth with the love, the joy, and the unity we have for each other. We can lean into His heart, face to face, and receive in order to release as we dance with Him.

John 5:17-20a
So Jesus explained himself at length. I'm telling you this straight. The Son can't independently do a thing, only what he sees the Father doing. What the Father does, the Son does. The Father loves the Son and includes him in everything he is doing. (The Message)

Jesus essentially told them He was simply following His Father's lead. Just like in dancing. The Father was doing a small dance at the Pool of Bethesda, hoping those gathered there would join in the celebration, but they didn't.

In another place, Jesus scolded his critics for not joining in the joy of what the Father was doing through Him: "We played the flute for you," Jesus said, and the great indictment of them was: "and you did not dance" (Luke 7:32). The old shaker song, written by Sydney Carter, takes the image Jesus used and extends it into a song.

> I danced for the scribe
>> And the Pharisee,
>> But they would not dance
>> And they wouldn't follow me.
>> I danced for the fishermen-
> For James and John-
>> They came with me
>> And the dance went on.
>> Dance, then, wherever you may be,
>> I am the Lord of the Dance, said he,
>> And I'll lead you all, wherever you may be,
>> And I'll lead you all in the Dance, said he.

In stepping to the rhythms of the waltz, I realized that I could only give away what I had first received. For me, the gesture of leaning back is an image of receiving; leaning forward, an image of giving. The image captures a rhythm of resting to receive, then releasing to give. Leaning back in rest, receiving what He has to give me. Leaning forward to release, giving what I have received to others.

Are you tired? Worn out? Burned out on religion? Come to Jesus! Get away with Jesus and you'll recover your life. He'll show you how to take a real rest. Walk with Him and work with Him and move with Him. Learn the unforced rhythms of grace. He won't lay anything heavy or ill-fitting on you. Keep company with Him and you'll learn to live freely and lightly.

Ephesians 5:18-19
And do not be drunk with wine, in which is dissipation; but be filled with the Spirit, speaking to one another in psalms and hymns and spiritual songs, singing and making melody in your heart to the Lord.

It is first a filling, then a spilling. For if we're not filled, we have nothing to give. We're ministering out of our emptiness rather than out of our fullness. First be filled, then empty yourself to others. Receive, and then give. Rest, and then release.

Mark 3:14
Jesus appointed the twelve so that they might be with Him.

Our activity for God is meant to flow rhythmically out of our intimacy with Him. Being "with Him" is how intimacy is cultivated. In the process of following Jesus as closely as they did, the disciples fell in love with Him. Once that happened, He began to send them out two-by-two, as partners in the dance.

Since the Holy Spirit revealed to me the rhythms of heaven are in the waltz, I have been dancing ever since. Now when I waltz, I often sing in time with the beat: "Re-ce-ive my joy...my joy, my joy. Be-ho-old my child...my child, my child." And the dance goes on. For a minute. For an hour. Sometimes two.

Questions for Personal Ponder or Group Discussion

1. Are you ready to roll, turn, and glide with your lover? In your own words, what does that look like to you?

2. Are you moving to the rhythm of heaven? Have you learned through soaking when to lean back and when to lean forward?

3. Who is leading you in your dance? Is it Father God or have you given His place to another person or material thing in your life?

4. Is your life in the need of recovery? If yes, elaborate.

5. Will you take the time to lean back and be filled so that you can lean forward and spill what you've received and bless those around you?

Activation

Meditate on the fathering love of God using the Scriptures mentioned in this chapter. Let them inspire you to gaze upon His beauty and majesty. Ask the Father to develop in you the heart of intimacy.

Gleanings in His Presence

CHAPTER 5

Resting is Receiving

*Intimacy brings us to the realm of blessing.
As we gaze upon the beauty of the Lord,
what is of Him and of His world permeates our being.*

The Realm of Blessing

Intimacy brings us to the realm of blessing. When Moses stayed before the Presence of God, his face shone with the very glory that he was exposed to- the glory of God. In the same way, as we gaze upon the beauty of the Lord, what is of Him and of His world permeates our being.

Psalm 63:5
You satisfy me more than the richest feast. I will praise you with songs of joy. (NLT)

The word *feast* here indicates a place of provision, fellowship, abundance and joy. In His Presence, we experience His fullness. Jesus came so we might have life and have it abundantly. This promise is available for us to experience here and now. This is the heart of our good Father; He wants to lavish us with His blessings and love.

Where God is, that is the realm of blessing.

Joseph, despite his predicament, prospered in all things because God was with him. As we abide in Him, being conscious and aware of His Presence constantly, He will remain in us. Where God is, that is the realm of blessing. The branch bears fruit in the place of abiding. The term fruits can be applied not only to spiritual things but also physical or material blessings. 3 John 1:2 says, *"Beloved, I pray that in all respects you may prosper and be in good health, just as your soul prospers."* Although this is not our motivation for soaking, blessings are indeed by-products of our encounters with God. Let me enumerate a number of blessings we receive from soaking prayer.

Spiritual refreshing and renewal
Isaiah 40:31
But they who wait for the LORD shall renew their strength; they shall mount up with wings like eagles; they shall run and not be weary; they shall walk and not faint. (ESV)

When we soak, spiritual renewal and refreshing come. The grace for today is not sufficient for tomorrow. Like manna, we need to access God's resources on a daily basis. We need to be filled again and again because we leak out as we go on with life.

Jesus demonstrated in His life the need to access heaven constantly. He would withdraw from the crowd to be alone with the Father. He needed supernatural strength to be able to minister again for another day. Remember, He ministered as a man completely dependent on the empowering of the Holy Spirit and the love of the Father. We can only minister from an overflow, so we need to be filled up time and time again. Soaking allows our hearts and soul to rest, be replenished and refilled.

Supernatural strength
Psalm 84:5-7
How blessed is the man whose strength is in You, in whose heart are the highways to Zion! Passing through the valley of Baca they make it a spring; the early rain also covers it with blessings. They go from strength to strength, every one of them appears before God in Zion.

When we soak, we are exchanging strength with God.

We live in a broken world and our spirit and soul are bombarded daily with its system and the enemy's evil schemes. When we spend time with God, we re-align our hearts again and again to His, lest we fall into the enemy's trap. The word *renew* in Hebrew means to exchange. When we soak, we are actually exchanging strength with God. It is His supernatural strength that gives us strength to stand firm and take the offensive against the enemy. We need His strength to run with our assignment and to soar in greater heights. It is this strength that will sustain us through the hustle and bustle of daily life. With His strength in and through us, we are able to carry out our Kingdom assignments with such affectivity, authority, boldness, confidence, and might.

Fresh revelation and knowledge of God
Isaiah 64:4
For from days of old they have not heard or perceived by ear, nor has the eye seen a God besides You, Who acts in behalf of the one who waits for Him.

Psalm 46:10
"Cease striving and know that I am God; I will be exalted among the nations, I will be exalted in the earth."

To cease striving is to be still. In stillness, God reveals new facets of His nature. When we allow our hearts to be quiet before Him, a fresh knowing of His essence and character comes. When we let go and let God, there are deeper realms we discover. It is in our stillness that He is able to bring us into the depths.

Hearing His Voice
Luke 10:42
"...for Mary has chosen the good part and it shall not be taken away from her."

Mary surely heard of the miracles of Jesus prior to this event, some of which she might even have witnessed herself. However, she was drawn more to the *person* who did the miracles than the miracles themselves. The opportunity to be with Jesus face to face, and hear His voice, is something she couldn't afford to miss. His Presence is far more important than the concerns of the moment. Mary chose the best part.

This a picture of what it is to tarry and remain at the feet of Jesus, waiting for every word that He says and to gaze at the beauty of His glory. As we draw near to God, He draws near to us, allowing us to hear and feel Him. God wants to speak to us the secrets and the longings of His heart. All we need to do is to rest at His feet and incline our ears to listen.

Being still at the feet of the Lord does not undermine genuine desires for the miraculous or passion to serve the Lord with great exploits. There is a time for deep intimacy and a time to exercise the authority and grace we received from His Presence. I believe it is important to understand we have to make the *one thing* the first thing. In soaking prayer, the one thing becomes the first thing.

Miracles, signs and wonders, or even blessings, should point us toward deeper encounters with God. They shouldn't take the place of our need and desire for His Presence. We can never "camp" on signs and focus on one particular manifestation and say, "This is it!" There's always more to discover and more to experience in His Presence. Martha did well, but Mary found what's best. Mary found deep encounters with the Son of God. Pause and imagine, what were the living words Mary heard from the very

God wants to speak to us the secrets and the longings of His heart. All we need to do is to rest at His feet and to incline our ear to listen.

lips of the One Who is the Beloved of the Father. Oh the depths of the wisdom of God, who can search and fathom His ways!

Sometimes what we know could hinder us from what we should know in the next season if we do not allow the Holy Spirit to direct our inner man. That's why we have to always open our hearts to hear like Mary, so we will be able to choose the very things that are of eternal significance, things that cannot be stolen from us. It is crucial that we are always current in the seasons of God so we will know what to do. And we can know it; if we keep a listening heart.

Increase in anointing, authority and spiritual power

The secret to spiritual power is the secret place. When you encounter God, the power in you increases. As you soak in His Presence, you are energized with His anointing, authority and power.

When we look at Moses in Exodus 3, we see God called Him to free the Israelites from the grip of the Pharaoh. He encountered God in the burning bush, and despite the awesome experience, he was still arguing the point that God chose him to speak to Pharaoh and deliver the nation of Israel from bondage. However when we look at him in Exodus 33, after several encounters with God, we see that Moses has been transformed. He was communing with God face to face as a man would a friend. At that point the level of authority, maturity, wisdom and favor upon his life had increased tremendously, he asked God boldly, *"Show me now Your glory!"* This time, his demeanor and confidence was completely opposite the first time he met God. Only a man intimately acquainted with God will have such confidence and boldness in His Presence. There is acceleration in spiritual growth as you progress in your encounters with God. Intimacy equals authority.

Freedom and breakthroughs

As the inner working of the power within us increases we overcome resistance and obstacles that come our way. This is how breakthrough in and through us takes place, and it is connected to our encounters with Him. Breakthrough is a significant and dramatic overcoming of obstacles, limitations, allowing a completion of a process and that moves you into a whole new level or state. In the Presence of God, the impossible becomes possible.

God is a god of breakthroughs. He was with Joshua when they first spied the land. As He was with Moses, He was with Joshua who became the leader He appointed to lead Israel to the Promise Land. It was a major breakthrough not just for Joshua but more so for the rest of the nation of Israel. I believe those moments Joshua spent with God prepared him for the shift in the season and state of the nation of Israel, from wandering around the desert into entering the Promise Land. God is faithful! He faithfully rewarded those times when Joshua would stay at the Door of the Tent of Meetings.

On the personal level, soaking brings us to the place of freedom, as Paul wrote, *"For where the Spirit of the Lord is, there is freedom."* (2 Corinthians 3:17, NIV) When the anointing comes upon us, it breaks the yoke of bondage. Habits and mindsets that are dealt with are radically changed in the secret place with God. One genuine encounter with God is so powerful it can break off the chains of bondage that the devil had put upon us. One revelation of Truth can expel lies and deceptions.

Blessings and abundance
Psalm 63:5
My soul is satisfied as with marrow and fatness, and my mouth offers praises with joyful lips.

Psalm 23:6
Surely goodness and lovingkindness will follow me all the days of my life, and I will dwell in the house of the Lord forever.

You don't need to chase the blessings; they will surely chase you when you constantly remain in His Presence. When we are filled with blessings, we overflow with blessings to others.

Ephesians 1:3
"Blessed be the God and Father of our Lord Jesus Christ, who has blessed us with every spiritual blessing in the heavenly places in Christ."

This verse is so pregnant with revelations. First, we have to understand from God's point of view, we are already blessed. It is a finished deal and at the same time it is an ongoing reality available for us to access. The spiritual blessing mentioned here covers all we need in this life. That's huge! However, we only get to access these blessings as we remain in Christ and be in the heavenly realm in the place of intimacy.

Questions for Personal Ponder or Group Discussion

1. Are your soaking motivations changing from wanting the blessings and fruit, to realizing that without that time with Him, you're spirit man could not survive?

2. Ask the Lord to reveal to you any "thing(s)" that need(s) to be removed from your spirit in order to allow yourself to be an empty vessel whose purpose is to be filled, spilled, and filled again.

3. Have you begun to understand through the rest of soaking God equips you with strength to target your assignment you have on your life? Explain.

4. What are the needs you have in your life, on a scale of most important to least important? Now ask yourself, "Is hearing His voice and seeking His presence even more important?"

5. Make a list of the secret blessings God has released into your life.

Activation

The Word of God says, "Delight yourself in the Lord and He will give you the desires of your heart" (Psalm 37:4). What concerns you concerns Him because you are valuable in His sight. In the place of delighting in Him, God releases His blessings and resources to make sure what brings us delight, our hopes, dreams and desires will come to pass. In this section, I invite you to rest in the Father's faithfulness and generosity. As your heart gaze upon His bigness and greatness, see your dreams and longings in the light of His willingness to bless you abundantly. Soak on His intentionality and unrelenting desire to bring you to the fullness of your call and destiny.

Gleanings in His Presence

CHAPTER 6

Beholding is Becoming

In God's sovereign plan He designed us to live in His Presence, and be filled with His very Presence and from that place we shine with His glory in all that we are and all that we do.

Face to Face

We are created for face-to-face encounters with God. Imagine the first time Adam opened his eyes at the very instance God breathed on his nostrils the breath of Life. In a moment, He saw the face of God shining in glory right in front of him! Just imagine, as he was gazing upon His face, all that God is- His love, power, goodness, majesty, perfection, and glory inundated him and every fiber of his being pulsated with divine life. Literally, Adam was saturated with God. He was soaked in glory!

This is a beautiful picture of what face-to-face with God looks like. This encounter was not just for Adam exclusively, but it is for the rest of mankind as well. In God's sovereign plan, He designed us, His Masterpiece, to live in His Presence, in the place of intimacy. This is our highest purpose for creation, to host and be filled with the very Presence of God and live in perfect union with the Godhead. From that place we shine with His glory in all we are and all we do.

God placed the first man and woman in the Garden He called Eden. Eden means pleasure and delight. He created a perfect world, and it was not enough, He planted a Garden, the Garden of His delight and pleasure which became the special home for His beloved masterpiece, the first man and woman. In the garden He gave them the mandate to manage the whole creation by expanding the borders of Eden to the rest of His created world.

We are God's bull's eye of His delight and eternal affection.

God, Who is love in highest perfection, sovereignly chose us to be at the very center of His delight and pleasure. We are God's bull's eye of His eternal affection. Mankind is created and wired for intimacy with the Maker.

Day after day, God would walk with Adam and Eve in the Garden in the cool of the day. As the days unfolded Adam and Eve discover the different facets of God's character and beauty. The more they saw Him and heard Him, the more they wanted to know Him, and the more they discovered who they were in Him. Gazing upon His face was like looking in the mirror; they saw their true identity in Him; for so they were primarily created in His image and likeness.

How we wish this beautiful story had never ended, but it did. Sin came in destroying this perfect picture of the love-relationship between God and His children in the Garden of His delight. The damage caused by the Fall was cataclysmic. Not only did sin come into mankind with its corresponding curse and death, the very image and likeness of God in man was disfigured and marred beyond recognition. The damage was not just something physical; it was deep within the recesses of man. His spirit was broken and paralyzed by sin. Together his soul and his body suffered the horrendous consequences of the Fall. Fallen mankind was separated from the Holy God for the first time. Fellowship was broken.

Thanks be to God, through Jesus everything was restored back to its original intent. Through Him we have been brought back to the Father's House to see His face and hear His voice again. Jesus became the Way, and the Door, back to the Father.

Discovering Eden Within

What was lost in the Garden has been restored in Christ, all of it. Although the fullness of the restoration process of all things back to Christ is ongoing, the price needed for its fulfillment had been paid in full. The moment Jesus shouted on the Cross, "It is finished!", those words resonated throughout all of eternity. It was sealed in heaven forever. The way has been established, the price paid, Mankind can now be reconciled with the Holy God. In Christ we are accepted, affirmed, loved and restored completely back to the Father's embrace. Once more, coming face-to-face with God is possible through Jesus and by the leading of the Holy Spirit Who Himself takes residence in us. This is amazing! This is the Good News of the Kingdom of God.

In Christ, we have been brought back to that place of intimacy with the Father, back to the Garden of Eden. Jesus, Who is the Beloved of the Father, has become unto us our Eden. As Adam and Eve were placed in the midst of the Garden of God's delight and pleasure, we have been placed and hidden in Christ. He will forever be God the Father's Delight and Pleasure, and so in Him we are too.

As Adam and Eve were placed in the midst of the Garden of God's delight and pleasure, we have been placed and hidden in Christ. He will forever be God the Father's Delight and Pleasure, and so in Him we are too.

In His death on the cross, Jesus became all that we are so in His resurrection and ascension we could become all He is to the Father.

Now, we are accepted in the Beloved Son. Therefore, we are equally loved, approved, and favored by the Father as His Begotten Son, Jesus. This is important revelation, because how we see God has so much to do with how we see ourselves, and vice versa and our view affects how we approach God. As we remain in living relationship with the Holy Spirit, we are brought to perfect fellowship and union between the Eternal Father and His Beloved Son from eternity to eternity. Christ in us is our Eden within. Because of Christ, the Father's eyes and affections are set on us.

Fruitfulness in Intimacy

The Parable of the Vine and the Branches in John 15 contains secrets to Kingdom lifestyle of fruitfulness, abundance, intimacy, authority, favor, joy and fullness of life. This parable outlines how we should live our lives on this earth as citizens of the Kingdom of God. In fact, the essence of our Christian life is captured in Jesus' words saying, "abide in Me and I will abide in you". This is what divine union is all about and it is only possible by the Holy

Spirit alone. We have the access to be in the Presence of God at all times by abiding and remaining in Jesus organically in a living, love relationship.

Intimacy brings us to the depths of God in Christ. What is true to Christ is true to us in that place. Just as the life-giving sap of the vine flows through all the branches, all the Life is in Christ flows through us as we remain in Him. Eternal fruits are natural by-products of this divine union with Him. These fruits are born out of the inner workings of the Holy Spirit in and through us as we respond in faith and obedience. These fruits lead to the expansion and demonstration of the Kingdom of God to the world around us. He is glorified when we bear much fruit, and our fruit remains. Fruits can be signs and wonders and miracles through us, or it can be breakthroughs, victories, exploits, creativity, wisdom, and all that's available from heaven to us as His children.

The fruit of our union with God in the secret place can be manifested in every aspect of our being. What happens in secret will be rewarded in the open. This goes beyond our responsibility and ministry in the church. It encompasses our spirit, our soul, and body. In the Old Testament, the Ark of the Covenant remained with the family of Obed-edom in his house for three months. "And the Lord blessed his family with all that he had." (1 Chronicles 13:14). The Ark is the only physical thing in the Old Testament that 'housed' the glorious Presence of God.

God's Presence brings blessings and fruitfulness. David confidently declared in the wilderness while Saul, driven by jealousy, was running after him to kill him, yet he said, "my soul is satisfied with marrow and fatness" (Psalm 63:5). The physical setting around him was contrary to this proclamation, but David was so assured of the blessings and the abundance of God coming his way. Why? Because God was with him and that he made His Presence his dwelling place and refuge. In Psalm 23 David wrote, "…surely, goodness and mercy shall follow me all the days of my life." How's that for boldness and confidence?

From Glory to Glory

In our face-to-face encounters with God, we are changed. What we behold we become. We can testify of the deep transformational impact soaking prayer has had on our lives. There are times when going deep into the Presence of God, the Holy Spirit comes and saturates us with His energy and virtue changing us from the inside out, putting our innermost being in proper place and state before God. Like a sponge He fills us, and at the same time He deals with and uproots things in our heart that are not in alignment with the Father and His Will. There are instances when, as we soaked in His Presence, we don't have the full understanding or even an ounce of a clue of what transpired in our encounter with Him. However, as we come out from our experience, we see changes happening in our lives, in our temperaments, desires, patience, characters, enhancing a deeper hunger for more of Him, increase in power, authority, wisdom, and a greater level of anointing upon us for service. It is impossible to be exposed to the glory of God and not be transformed.

In 2 Corinthians 3:18 Paul wrote, "But we all, with unveiled face beholding as in a mirror the glory of the Lord, are being transformed (Gk. metamorphosis) into the same image from glory to glory, just as from the Lord, the Spirit". This verse is filled with blessings and promises that we are to receive in our face-to-face encounter with God. Measures of change can be achieved with discipline and practice. However, nothing can compare to the transformation brought about by deep encounters with God. In our ongoing journeys into the presence of God we find nuggets of insights from this verse.

Throughout the whole chapter Paul described the comparison between the ministry of the Spirit we now have in Christ with the ministry of the letter or the law Moses lived in. He wrote that whenever the Law is read a veil covers the hearts of the sons of Israel. However, whenever a man turns to the Lord, the veil is lifted. So, in Christ and by the Holy Spirit, we come face-to-face with God with unveiled face and a wide-opened heart. This is an awesome privilege we have by the Spirit of God.

This is the starting point. We come to the Father without shame or condemnation knowing we are accepted in Him because we are in Christ. The Father wants to make Himself known to us because we are His children. He loves to display His goodness and His glory upon us, as we respond with our hearts open, yielded, and transparent to His inner working.

We look to Him, we behold His glory and in that place, like a man looking in a mirror, we also see our image in Him. And that image will always be glorious.

As we gaze upon His face with unveiled hearts, we behold His glory as in a mirror. This is an amazing truth. As we look to Him, we behold His glory and in that place, like a man looking in a mirror, we also see our image in Him, and that image will always be glorious. Beholding the glory of God and His attributes, His character, His goodness and greatness, awakens and energizes our whole being. We will become more alive in His Presence, and we find the best of who we are in Him.

The word transformation in this verse means metamorphosis. The best illustration in biology for this process would be a destructive caterpillar transforming into a beautiful butterfly. In the Presence of God, as we see His glory and discover who we are in Him, we are being metamorphosized into His likeness from glory to glory. What we behold we become.

Jesus said, "If you have seen Me, then you have seen the Father". This is more than just likeness in physical appearance. It is the essence, the Divine Nature in Jesus that demonstrated His likeness and oneness with the Father. This is our destiny. By the Holy Spirit, and in the Presence of the Father, we are being conformed into the likeness of Christ.

Deeper Dealings

The psalmist wrote "deep calls to deep…" (Psalm 42:7). As we rest and are still in the Presence of God, the Holy Spirit goes deep in the recesses of our being. With our hearts and minds unveiled before Him, He comes not just to encourage and refresh us, He also comes to deal with us and do the necessary work within us.

As the Vinedresser, the Father prunes us to remove the good and make way for the best things- greater fruitfulness and abundance in Him.

There are times He comes as the Great Physician doing deep surgery in us removing the decays, the fears, offenses and issues that hinder us from experiencing the fullness of our destiny and our inheritance as His beloved sons and daughters. He uses the scalpel of His Word to cut deep into our hearts, intentions, and ambitions. As the Vinedresser, the Father prunes us to remove the good and make way for the best things, greater fruitfulness and abundance in Him. He chisels off the rugged edges in our lives to bring about the real treasures in us.

Given the choice, we should rather have the hands of the loving Father deal with us and shape us in the secret place than for anyone who is void of love do it. Moving to greater levels in the Spirit requires us to let go of things that hinder us, and make way for greater things God has for us. In the Presence of our loving Father, letting go of our issues, fears, excuses and struggles becomes the most natural thing to do. There's no need to have our arms twisted on this one. Remember, He is good.

Questions for Personal Ponder or Group Discussion

1. Has your relationship or "fellowship" with God been broken or limited by sin? If so, allow Him to restore those broken pieces so that you can be brought back into fellowship with Him.

2. Who do you see when you look in the mirror? Who does God say you are?

3. As you begin to soak, allow yourself to go deeper in intimacy with Father God! Begin to make note of all the circumstances He's brought you through, and all the new boldness and confidence you will begin to experience so that the next time you are facing a challenging circumstances, you can reflect on those past examples of God's goodness.

4. Do you have shame or condemnation in your life? How can you overcome that shame and guilt?

5. Are you ready to let go of the hindrances in your life? If yes, begin to ask God to show you the troubled, broken, fearful areas that He is going to mend and heal.

Activation

Try extending your soaking time at this point. Begin by asking the Holy Spirit to lead you into deep encounters with the facets of God's Nature. Be sensitive to what He shows you and keep your heart yielded and longing for more. The deeper you go in your desire for more of Him, the deeper He comes. Pray that He would do the necessary inner workings in your heart and desire deeply that you would be transformed into His image and likeness. Write down what you have received from your encounter with Him.

Gleanings in His Presence

CHAPTER 7

The Royal Priesthood

As priests, we are called to minister to God in the secret place. As kings, we have the covering of authority and favor of the Father upon us and by the power of the Holy Spirit we expand the Kingdom of God.

1 Peter 2:9
But you are a chosen race, a royal priesthood, a holy nation, a people for God's own possession, so that you may proclaim the excellencies of Him who has called you out of darkness into His marvelous light.

Revelation 5:9-10
And [now] they sing a new song, saying, You are worthy to take the scroll and to break the seals that are on it, for You were slain (sacrificed), and with Your blood You purchased men unto God from every tribe and language and people and nation. And You have made them a kingdom (a royal race) and priests to our God, and they shall reign [as kings] over the earth! [AMP]

We were not saved just to have a ticket to heaven and in the meantime to maintain selfless and sinless lives here on earth. The purpose of our calling is to make known the excellencies of God. We are called to reveal and demonstrate His power, goodness, and love. We are destined to bring heaven here on earth.

The term 'royal priesthood' signifies that we are both to be priests and kings before our God. In the Old Testament the priests focused on intercession and serving God in worship, and the offering of sacrifices in the secret place, while kings focus on ruling and reigning by decrees over their domains. Our identity as royal priesthood is crucial, because we are called to walk in a balance of these two aspects of our identity.

As priests, we are called to minister to God in the secret place. In intimacy we see His face and hear His voice. As kings, we have the covering of authority and favor of the Father upon us, and by the power of the Holy Spirit we expand the Kingdom of God. We rule by serving the people in love and destroying the works of the enemy. What we have received in the secret place, in the ministry of the priest, we are to release to the world, destroy the works of the enemy, and dispense the resources of heaven as kings. This is how we are to declare and show forth His excellencies and glory to this earth.

Receiving is Reigning

Romans 5:17
For if by the transgression of the one, death reigned through the one, much more those who receive the abundance of grace and of the gift of righteousness will reign in life through the One, Jesus Christ.

One of the precious principles we need to remember in this life is: everything in the Kingdom of God is to be received, not achieved. In addition to this, we cannot release what we have not received. In Matthew 10:1 it says, " And having summoned His twelve disciples, He gave them authority over unclean spirits, to cast them out, and to heal every kind of disease and every kind of sickness." The Twelve received authority in the Presence of Jesus as He commissioned them to do the works of the Kingdom. And Jesus went on to say, "freely you received, freely give." We cannot release or give what we have not received from Him. The measure in which we receive from Him in the secret place is the same measure in which we are able to release to the world.

> *Everything in the Kingdom of God is to be received, and not to be achieved.*

Jesus sits at the right hand of the Father as Priest and King in the heavens. In the Old Testament, the priest who ministered in the secret place sat down to rest only when he had finished offering up sacrifices to the Lord. In the same way, a king who is ruling over his domain sits on his throne. Both pictures reveal the meaning of Jesus' place in the heavenlies, sitting at the right hand of the Father. As the High Priest in the heavens, He completed the sacrifice necessary for the redemption of mankind, and He's been given all the power and authority in heaven and on earth and now He sits on the throne ruling and reigning as the King of kings and the Lord of lords.

From the verse above we see that our measure of receiving from heaven is the measure of our reigning in life. This is an important key in living out the Kingdom lifestyle. Heaven is the model and the pattern for earth. Jesus taught His disciples to pray,

"Let Your Kingdom come, let Your Will be done, on earth as it is in heaven." As priests, ministering before God in worship and intercession in the secret place, we receive from heaven the very answers that would address the needs here on earth.

Our measure of receiving from heaven is the measure of our reigning in life.

The Kingdom of God is the total answer to the total needs of man. Jesus made the way for us to access heaven and live in its reality in the Spirit and be able to experience our inheritance as sons of God here and now. Through Him we have access to the heavenly resources needed to transform this earth and make it look just like heaven. We received what Jesus accomplished, the finished work of the cross, by faith in the place of intimacy. In a race, we start from the starting line, but in Christianity we start from the finish line, the finished work of Jesus. That's why Christian life is all by faith and grace.

After receiving from heaven, we are to rule and reign here on earth, exercising the authority given to us. We have been commissioned to destroy the works of darkness, and set the captives free. We take every land for our King and expand the borders of His Kingdom as we go and proclaim the Good News. We bring His Presence to the widows and orphans, the last, the lost, the least, the forsaken and the sick. We mark people for blessing and declare over them their destiny that God has for them.

Jesus modeled the priestly and kingly lifestyle. Both aspects are essential to us walking this earth because "as He is so are we in this world." He said I only say what I hear my Father say, I only do what I see my Father do. This is the lifestyle that we are called to live. This is Jesus' secret - His hidden life with the Father. In the same way, as priests, we should see and hear God first so we can go and do. We must be good receivers of His realm as priests so as kings we can release heaven's resources with all authority to address the needs around us.

Kingdom Priests and Kings

Luke 5:15-16
But the news about Him was spreading even farther, and large crowds were gathering to hear Him and to be healed of their sicknesses. But Jesus Himself would often slip away to the wilderness and pray.

This is a picture of how Jesus walked as a priest and as a king before God. In the midst of all the demands and business around Jesus, He was sensitive to the gentle nudges of the Holy Spirit. He would go to a solitary place to be with the Father. The word *often* from the verse above signifies not an act done intermittently, but an act done repeatedly and regularly, which develops a lifestyle. Soaking in the Presence of the Father is part of who He is.

Great multitudes came to Him and he would preach to them and heal them. As a King, He released the authority of heaven and destroyed the works of the enemy – healing the sick, casting out demons, and raising the dead. He did not just teach them good lessons about the Kingdom; He demonstrated the truth and led them to experience the truth.

Like Christ, we have to walk as priests and kings before God in carrying out our mandate to bring heaven on earth. We have to minister from an overflow of what we receive in the secret place. Burning out is the result of ministering beyond the level of what we have received.

2 Samuel 6:14-15
And David was dancing before the LORD with all his might, and David was wearing a linen ephod. So David and all the house of Israel were bringing up the ark of the LORD with shouting and the sound of the trumpet.

An ephod is the prescribed sacred vestment worn only by the high priest as they minister before the Lord in the Old Testament times. David was already king of Israel when this particular event happened. His desire to bring the Ark of the Covenant into his city was unwavering. Despite the failure in the first attempt during which Uzzah died as he tried to *help* the Ark and accidentally touched it, David's passion to bring the Presence of God in the midst of his people had been his deepest desire. He ached for God to inhabit whole nation of Israel and not just visit His people.

David was a pursuer of God's heart and we see from this verse that as a king, he led the procession of people bringing the Ark of the Covenant that housed the Manifest presence of God into his city. In the presence of his people, David danced with all of his might because finally, what he ached for, the longing of his heart, the presence of God would remain and stay in the midst of Israel.

Imagine, a mighty warrior dancing with all of his might before God. That must be one raw, passionate display of intense, wild, high praise to Jehovah God because He is greatly to be praised. This was a great praise offered to his great God and King. One more thing, David stripped himself of any vestments of royalty, although he was the newly crowned king. He was wrapped with an ephod, a priestly garb worn by the high priests offering up sacrifices unto the Lord. This very act revealed to everyone the core of his being: it is intimacy with God and creating a habitation for God to dwell. We see later in David's life this desire was the very thing that defined him more than any other thing.

It was not his throne that he was after; it was the manifest presence of God in between the cherub and the Mercy Seat, the place where God promised Moses to meet him face to face. It was the Throne of God that he sought for. Intimacy with God more than earthly authority is what he was chasing after. David wanted the people of Israel to experience and encounter God like he did. Although he was not a priest by office, because he did not belong to the tribe of Levites, he was a priest by his heart unto God. In a way, before he became a king over Israel, he was first a priest to God in the secret place.

Towards Greater Glory

Romans 11:33-36
Oh, the depth of the riches both of the wisdom and knowledge of God! How unsearchable are his judgments, and unfathomable His ways! Who has known the mind of the Lord? Or who has became his counselor? Or who has first given to Him that it might be paid back to Him again? For from Him and through Him and to Him are all things. To Him be the glory forever! Amen.

God never intended for our lives to be one great roller coaster ride up and down and turn around. He intended for us to go from one level of glory to another, and to another, and on towards the fullness of Christ Jesus. This is the standard He has for all of us. Many times we lower the standard based on our level of experience instead of adjusting our experiences to the level of His intentions and desires for us He revealed in His Word.

Jesus is the standard of God. His life gives us a clear picture of how it is to live a life fully surrendered to the will of the Father and 100% dependent on the empowering of the Holy Spirit. Everything that Jesus is and did came from the Father. If that's the way He did it, then what better way could we do except to allow Christ in us live out the same lifestyle through us.

All things are from Him! All matters about the Kingdom, and all the works and resources must come from Him because He is the only source; through Him because He is the strength; and for Him because He is the sole purpose for everything and He is the only object of our devotion and worship. We have to get it from Him, everything we need in life. We have to depend upon His empowering, the power of the Holy Spirit working in and through us, and bring everything back to Him all for His glory! The increase and maturity come as we make these steps our lifestyle, from Him, through Him and for Him, to the glory of God. This is the way to go from glory to greater glory.

Sweet Surrender

Romans 12:1-2
Therefore, I urge you, brothers, in view of God's mercy, to offer your bodies as living sacrifices, holy and pleasing to God—this is your spiritual act of worship. Do not conform any longer to the pattern of this world, but be transformed by the renewing of your mind. Then you will be able to test and approve what God's will is—his good, pleasing and perfect will.(NIV)

From the verses above, we see Paul exhorting us how we should live our lives here on earth. To do that, it is crucial to offer up our lives as living sacrifices before God. We could view this scenario like something bloody and gory, like a lamb being slaughtered and disemboweled and cut open. As we read from the previous chapter, we come to understand the essence of the sacrifice Paul was referring to here. A careful reading of the last few verses from chapter 11 reveals the tone is nowhere near a slaughterhouse, but a very encouraging and inviting place of exchange. God knows everything and no one could fathom His wisdom and all things are from Him, through Him and for Him. With this in view, we see an invitation was given to surrender everything to Him who is the Greatest, the Highest and the sovereign One who has all things in place.

Before God, the place of surrender is the place of exchange.

Paul invites us to live holy lives, yielded to God's will completely and making our lives an offering of worship to the Lord. The place of surrender is the place of exchange. As we surrender, we are actually trading our frailty for His strength, our foolishness for His wisdom, and our ashes for His garland of beauty. All that's ours for all that's His. How's that for an exchange deal? What a wonderful invitation from heaven. The more we surrender and yield our faculties to Him, the more we receive what is of Him and from Him. This is what we call "sweet surrender".

Going up to the Mountain

Matthew 14 tells us a very difficult time in Jesus' ministry. In verse thirteen, we read about how John's disciples came to Him and reported what happened to His cousin, John the Baptist, who was beheaded and buried. Let's observe how Jesus handled the situation.

He withdrew to a lonely place by Himself. Mourning the death of His cousin, He knew full well the time of His death was drawing near. This is a time of intense grief and pressure. Like an olive, the moment the squeezing began, the oil started to come out. He knew where to go – to be alone with the Father. Once more we see Jesus all by Himself, receiving courage and strength from the Father.

As He was contemplating in an isolated place, the multitudes knew about it and they followed Him. He saw them and had compassion on them. Right after He heard the bad news about John the Baptist, and barely finished drawing strength from heaven, He was moved with compassion the moment He saw the multitudes. In the following verse we see Him healing their sicknesses until evening. Where did He get such depth of strength and compassion? For sure, it could never be from this world, but from the superior world of His Father - the Kingdom of Heaven.

Jesus never lost His focus, or His timing in the midst of anguish and great needs. In fact this was the very situation in which He multiplied the bread and fish and fed five thousands of men, aside from women and children. What kind of heart beats like that? Although He needed rest, He chose to give rest to the weary. Instead of mourning, He comforted the lost and the lonely. What spurred Him on like that? It was the love of the Father. He was drawing everything from the heart of the Father. The Father provided Him strength, grace, and anointing needed for that particular hour.

After feeding the multitudes, He told His disciples to get into the boat go ahead of Him to the other side as He sent the multitudes away. At that point, it was very late at night. In verse twenty-three it says, "And after He had sent the multitudes away, He went up to the mountain by Himself to pray; and when it was evening, He was there alone." He went to the mountain by Himself to pray. This is a profound picture of the ultimate priority of Jesus, which was to be with the Father. We don't know how high was the mountain that He climbed, or how far it was from the place He did the multiplication of bread, but one very obvious thing is Jesus was compelled by something greater than His need for rest. What was it? It was the Love of the Father. It was to be in the presence of the Father and to hear His voice and see His face.

Coming from His encounter with the Father at the mountain, Jesus walked on the water in the fourth watch (3-6AM) to join His disciples on the boat! This is amazing. Let's pause for a while. We should see something powerful here. Jesus literally moved from one level of glory to another, and to another. Let's outline it carefully.

On hearing John the Baptist was beheaded, He went alone and pulled strength and encouragement from heaven. Next, He saw the multitudes and He was moved by compassion and He healed them all. Then, it was late at night and the people had nowhere to go to eat. He looked to heaven, again pulling the resources available from that superior world, the Kingdom of God, and gave thanks to the Father. The bread and the fish multiplied and everyone was fed, and twelve baskets of leftovers were gathered. Next, He sent the disciples and the multitudes away and once more He went to a mountain to be with the Father. From His encounter with the Father on the mountain, He came down and He walked on the water! He did it for no apparent reason. He brought so much of the Father's Kingdom with Him coming down from the mountain, so much so, Peter was able to walk on the water at His Word just like Jesus had.

How do you move from one glory to another? Move from receiving to releasing and going back again in His

From Him, through Him, and all for Him. This is Royal Priesthood ministry.

Presence to receive more, and to be able to release more. Remember this: From Him, through Him, and all for Him. This is Royal Priesthood ministry.

The Power of Declaration

How do we release the Kingdom of God in our midst or over situations? Under the power of the Holy Spirit, we will see the Kingdom of God released by decrees and declarations. This is how kings rule over their domains, through decrees and declarations. This is how we operate as royalty.

In Matthew 10:1-15, Jesus called His twelve and commissioned them to proclaim the Good News of the Kingdom, to heal the sick, cast out demons, cleanse lepers and raise the dead. They were to release or give what they had received from Him. He said, "freely you received freely you give." How do you think these bunch of disciples received it from Him in the first place? Did He give them badges or pins saying, "I have been appointed and anointed by heaven"? They received it from Jesus through prophetic prayers and declarations He spoke over them. He released authority and power to heal the sick, cleanse the lepers, raise the dead and proclaim the Good News of the Kingdom by declaring over them the commission of heaven in the same way that He had been commissioned by the Father. God the Father made declarations over Jesus as He was being baptized saying, "This is My Beloved Son in whom I am well-pleased." Further on, after Jesus finished fasting for forty days and forty nights and overcoming the devil, He went to Galilee and then to His hometown Nazareth. In the synagogue He read from the book of Isaiah saying:

"The Spirit of the Lord is upon Me, because He has anointed Me to preach the Gospel to the poor. He has sent Me to proclaim release to the captives, and recovery of sight to the blind, To set free those who are downtrodden, To proclaim the Favorable Year of the Lord."(Isaiah 61:1-2)

Jesus announced in the hearing of all, in heaven and on earth, the very purpose of His coming here on earth. In that declaration, the Kingdom of God was released. From that proclamation, we see the expansion of the Kingdom of God everywhere invading lives, cities, villages and societies.

Jesus announced in the hearing of all, in heaven and on earth, the very purpose of His coming here on earth. In that declaration the Kingdom of God has been released.

In the same way, Jesus instructed the twelve to release the Kingdom of God by declaration. How? In verse seven Jesus says, "As you go, preach (proclaim, declare) 'The Kingdom of heaven is at hand.'" Furthermore He told them in verse twelve and thirteen, *"And as you enter the house give it your greeting (proclamation, declaration of Peace). And if the house is worthy, let your greeting of peace come upon it; but if it is not worthy, let your greeting of peace return to you."*

The Kingdom of God is "righteousness, peace, and joy in the Holy Spirit." As we declare 'peace' over circumstances, the realm of the Kingdom is released, and then peace comes a tangible reality, it's not just a word. What we hear and received in the secret place as we soak in the presence of God, we are able to release by declaration.

Here's one unforgettable experience that illustrates our identity as a royal priesthood unto the Lord and releasing the excellencies and the glory of God in the darkest of places by declaration that took place in April 2009.

A team from Destiny Ministries International church joined some of the leaders and members of Hosanna Lutheran Church of Lakeville, Minnesota to minister to the pastors and leaders and conduct a four-night crusade in Jalna, Maharashtra India. The city has approximately 2 million in population, the majority of which are Hindus and Muslims. The last time the city had experienced a crusade was in 1994. Needing a fresh move of God, the leaders rose up in unity as they found hope when they heard the testimonies of the mighty deeds of God in the crusades we did in Ahmednagar the year before. Denominational barriers crumbled down as they rallied the Christians towards one goal - expanding the Kingdom of God in their city.

The highlights of the events centered on the revelation of the Father's Love, His family here on earth, Kingdom Alignment for Kingdom Assignment, and the Kingdom of God. As a whole, everything that happened validated the prophetic promise of God in Malachi 4:5-6 that says, *"See, I will send you the prophet Elijah before that great and dreadful day of the Lord comes. He will turn the hearts of the fathers to their children, and the hearts of the children to their fathers; or else I will come and strike the land with a curse."*

When the fathering spirit of Elijah comes, there is a tremendous impartation that happens in the presence of 'Elishas', sons who are hungry for the things of God and who would be willing to go through the process needed to lay hold of their inheritance. There is a release of a double-portion anointing that will give rise to the invasion of Heaven on Earth. We had no clue as to what we were about to witness in Jalna in the light of this revelation. Despite the concerns of our safety by the local police force, and the possibility of threats from some fundamentalist groups and the sensitivity of time because of the upcoming national election, we saw the mighty hand of God orchestrating everything for His glory. Everything that happened was indeed far more than what we had asked for or imagined.

The event started with a powerful meeting with the pastors and leaders of the city. Tim Hatt laid the foundation for the upcoming events. He shared a powerful message on the family of God, emphasizing the necessity of understanding the unity in the spirit despite our differences in the external things because we have one Father, one Holy Spirit and one Jesus. Tim also shared we belong to one Family and one Kingdom. After the word we asked the local leaders to lay their hands on the whole team and asked them to release favor in their land so we could freely minister to their people.

It was a sight to behold; the unity of the brethren of different color, race, age, gender, and denomination.

We were advised to leave the city on the first day of the crusade because of the sensitive situation. Upon hearing this, the team gathered and we started to soak in the presence of God. We opened wide our hearts and made room for His presence to come. In a moment, His presence became so thick in the room. As we moved deeper into the presence of God, the Lord gave a word from Psalm 144 that says, "Praise be to the Lord my Rock, who teaches my hands for war, my fingers for battle." I exhorted the whole team to take our stand in the spirit and we started to release declarations and decrees.

At that juncture, as Jon Borde, the Indian leader from Hosanna, who was overseeing all of the events, was prayed for, he fell under the power of God. Then he was asked to release prophetic declarations over Jalna and against the current situation we were facing. Like a mighty Kingdom warrior, he stood up and boldly proclaimed prophetic decrees and prayers while the rest of us agreed in unity. We felt a strong release in the spirit and some of the team members saw visions of what was happening in the spiritual realm as Jon spoke prophetic declarations. The Kingdom of God was released over the city by declaration.

Within a few minutes after our corporate soaking, we received the word from the police we would be allowed to stay overnight and be at the crusade ground to witness the event from the sideline. The Indian local leaders stood on the platform and they took charge of the event. It was a bold step of victory!

God opened the doors for us to continue pouring into the pastors and the church leaders. A small group of around thirty pastors and Bible school students gathered to listen as we continued to exhort them to take their stand and dig the wells of revival for their city. This exhortation included the supremacy, the nature and the access we have to the Kingdom of God. It was particularly emphasized they could pull or put a demand on the Kingdom of God by their desire because His Kingdom is very near. They were encouraged to get what they needed from the Kingdom of God and receive the answers in their hearts by faith. In the same way, they were to receive from heaven and then release to the people around them, especially during the crusade. They were so excited as they had learned to receive and then to release the Kingdom of God.

In the afternoon the team gathered again to pray for the second night of the campaign. Once more we soaked deep into the presence of God allowing the Holy Spirit to saturate us with His glory. It was a powerful time. The entire team united in the spirit to intercede on behalf of the city. We sensed a powerful release of the Spirit of God as we released the word of God on the breaker anointing and turn-around anointing we were going to witness in the crusade that night.

There was a sense of openness in the crusade and around 5,000 people showed up on the second night. Even during the worship time, the Spirit of the Lord was moving powerfully and people are being set free from demonic oppression. Pastor Sanjay, a Methodist pastor from Mumbai, who had been our faithful interpreter the previous year in Ahmednagar, released prophetic decrees and declarations over the people. He was instructed to release the prayers for sick people and deliverance over the microphone. On the stage, he spoke with authority and passion and commanded healing and deliverance. We heard loud shouts, and shrieks as hundreds were delivered from demonic spirits. There were breakthroughs everywhere as healings spontaneously happened, even outside the prayer lines. Many people came forward giving testimonies, and all of us shouted in celebration as we heard the first healing...a blind woman received her sight. Thereafter, almost every minute someone testifies on the platform speaking of the great things God did.

On the third night, the crowd increased to about 9,000 because of the testimonies of the mighty things that happened the night before. We left Jalna the following day filled with joy and celebration. We had accomplished our assignment in Jalna - releasing the Kingdom of God, standing shoulder to shoulder with the locals, and releasing impartation, anointing and revelation to them. One of the local leaders testified almost one hundred people received healing from different levels of blindness, and many were released from demonic oppression. We were told the crowd swelled to almost 12,000 that night. The good news is we were not there to do it, but the Elishas, the local leaders, were the ones who stepped out expanding the Kingdom of God in their land. They experienced receiving and releasing heaven over their city and seeing the supremacy of the Kingdom of God in confronting the works of the darkness around them. The seeds of transformation have been sown in that region and the Kingdom of God is mightily advancing! (Excerpt from my newsletter released in the same year.)

Questions for Personal Ponder or Group Discussion

1. Are you embracing the truth of being chosen? How will this new revelation of authority and royalty change the way you "do" ministry and live your life?

2. Have you ever felt burned out? What do you feel led to your burn out?

3. How high is your level of expectation? Is your expectation based on your experience, or God's intentions and desires for you?

4. Are you learning that through "sweet surrender" you are soaking up God's strength and compassion and from that you are able to leak out His goodness and touch people's lives?

5. What are some words God has given you to declare over your ministry, family, work, etc.? Begin to declare His words over your life and situations.

Activation

Receiving and releasing, that's the rhythm of heaven. Once more as you soak, allow God to overwhelm you with His Nature. Be aware and be sensitive in what He is doing within you and continually ask the Holy Spirit for insights and directions. The first part of your soaking would be on receiving and allowing Him to fill you. The next part would be to release the realm of heaven by your declarations. Your declarations should be according to what He brings to your mind and heart as you speak. Sense the release in the atmosphere as you do it. Another part of this activation is to ask Him for specific circumstances or individuals that He wants you to minister to. This is going to be an exciting exercise. You would be surprised at the simplicity of the Kingdom of God as you learn to receive and release the reality of heaven.

Gleanings in His Presence

_____
_____
_____
_____
_____
_____
_____
_____

CHAPTER 8

Inquiring at His Temple

We can never separate our Kingdom assignment from our Kingdom identity as sons and daughters of God. As we go deeper in intimacy, we discover who we are in Him and what He has called us to do and to be.

Psalm 27:4
"One thing I have desired of the Lord, that I will seek; that I may dwell in the house of the Lord all the days of my life, to behold the beauty of the Lord, and to inquire of His temple."

Gazing at His beauty and inquiring in His temple, both aspects of our coming to God are important. One might think that soaking prayer is only about developing intimacy with God. However, Psalm 27:4 reveals soaking prayer is not just about developing intimacy with God, although that should be our main motivation; it is also inquiring of Him about our Kingdom assignment.

We can never separate our Kingdom assignment or heavenly call (what we are called to do) from our Kingdom identity (who we are) as sons and daughters of God. As we go deeper in intimacy, we discover who we are in Him and what He has called us to do and to be. When John the Baptist saw Jesus by the River Jordan he exclaimed, "Behold, the Lamb of God Who takes away the sins of the world." The Lamb of God is Jesus' Kingdom identity, taking away the sins of the world is His Kingdom assignment.

The leadership of David differs from Saul's in so many ways. One difference was in the area of inquiring of the Lord. Saul inquired of God only once or twice throughout his reign as a king. David inquired of God in almost all of His battles. God revealed to him strategies and specific directions which brought him sure victories. David inquired of his assignment and he received the full backing of heaven as he went to lead Israel in possessing the Promise Land.

In 2 Samuel 5:17-25 we see that David inquired of the Lord twice before he and his army went to battle to face the Philistines. The first time was in verse 19 which states, *'So David inquired of the Lord, saying, 'Shall I go up against the Philistines? Will You deliver them into my hand?' And the Lord said to David, 'Go up, for I will doubtless deliver the Philistines into your hand.'* Despite his skills and great army, David took time to ask God and never presumed anything. The victory was sure, of course. He declared that God had broken through the Philistines before him like the breakthrough of waters.

The second time that he inquired of the Lord was when the Philistines once again came against Israel in Rephaim. Remember, earlier David wrought a great victory against the same nation. It would be an easy and logical step to go against their opponent at once considering the advantage they had over them, but David took time to inquire of the Lord. This shows his heart to trust God in all things, more than his strength or the size of his army. In verses twenty-three and twenty-four God gave David clear instruction on how to defeat the Philistines. God said, "You shall not go directly up; circle around behind them and come at them in front of the balsam trees. And it shall be, when you hear the sound of marching in the tops of the balsam trees, then you shall act promptly, for then the Lord will have gone out before you to strike the army of the Philistine."

It takes a listening heart to hear such a detailed instruction from the Lord. Such was David's heart; it was so trained and sensitive to the Voice of God. His heart was always leaning towards Him to listen. He developed this ability of recognizing God's voice through the intimate times he had with Him in the secret place. The instruction God gave him this time around was a complete opposite of the first one. The first one was a direct assault. This time around, they had to go behind the enemy and wait for the go signal, the sound of marching in tops of the balsam trees, before they fought their enemies. This is amazing! This time the angelic warriors marching on the balsam trees are with David and his army. To top it all off, God Himself went before them and strike the Philistines.

As we come into deep intimacy with God, more and more we capture His very heart and His mind and understand His purposes on earth and the very things He is about to do. He reveals His secrets to His friends because He desires for them to be part of the fulfillment of His plans on earth. The way to co-labor with God is to be able to recognize and hear His voice clearly, and to obey what He says. Hearing God's voice is imperative in our stepping into our destiny.

Soak for Work

Ephesians 2:10
"For we are His workmanship, created in Christ Jesus for good works, which God prepared beforehand, that we should walk in them."

There are Kingdom works appointed for us to do. The good thing is, it's a finished work. In fact, the Father has long prepared these good works for us to walk in, to enter. We come into His work by faith. This is a powerful revelation, but how do we enter in His finished works?

Hebrews 4:9-11 says, "There remains therefore a Sabbath rest for the people of God. For the one who has entered His rest has himself also rested from his works, as God did from His. Let us therefore be diligent to enter that rest, lest anyone fall through following the same example of disobedience." From these verses we see the key to entering His finished work is to be diligent to enter His rest. To do that, we must cease from striving, from the efforts of the flesh, and be in the place of rest, which is to have our faith anchored on the finished work of Jesus.

> *We work while resting and resting while working!*

So we see in the Kingdom of God, resting in His Presence is doing His works. We work while resting and rest while working! Soaking prayer should always bring us to a deeper awareness that Jesus indeed is the Finished Work of the Father, and the Father has prepared for us the good works we have been called to do.

In Acts 13:1-3 the leaders at Antioch ministered to the Lord and fasting and the Holy Spirit said, "Set apart for Me Barnabas and Saul for the work to which I have called them." As they were ministering to God, He gave them specific instruction to send Saul and Barnabas for the very work that He has called them to do. We know that after this the leaders sent the two and commissioned them to spread the Good News to the nations beyond.

Face to Face with the Creative God

Creativity inside of man is awakened and heightened in the presence of the Creative God. More and more we are seeing the release of creative ideas to people who have had deep encounters with Him. Countless songs we hear in our generation bear the thumbprints of genuine encounters with God. More and more we are seeing fresh ideas, creations, designs, colors, textures, tastes, movements, music and rhythms coming forth because of individuals who are exploring the depths of God in the secret place. What they see in secret, they are now empowered to display in the open for His glory!

More and more we are seeing fresh ideas, creations, designs, colors, textures, tastes, movements, music and rhythms are coming out because of individuals who are exploring the depths of God in the secret place.

Recently, we saw some major breakthroughs in the businesses of some of our members in Destiny Ministries International. If you ask them what their secret was, they will always point to their encounters with God as they learned to stay in His Presence through soaking prayer. There are new business ideas coming forth, strategic alliances, and supernatural connections happening because of the presence of God. There is a release of tremendous favor and open doors to those whose Kingdom assignments are in the marketplace. Not to mention the promotions, bonuses and increased influence several of our people have experienced after they have been to the presence of God. As our people learned to be good receivers in the secret place, they began to access the finished work of God.

There are several businesses that some of our people have launched out of the ideas God has shown them as they were soaking before His presence. One particular business is EnglishWorld, a Filipino company that envisions being the best English tutorial to non-English speaking nations especially in Asia. This business came as a heavenly download to Edwin Pages, a spiritual son whose assignment is in the marketplace. Within three years of its launching, it is now spreading to different Southeast Asian nations, and is currently setting up an internet-based English tutorial service that will cater primarily to Japanese and Korean clients, with many more nations on the horizon.

Questions for Personal Ponder or Group Discussion

1. Have you begun to discover who you are in Christ? If so, ask Father to reveal your assignment to you.

2. Are you able to hear God's voice and direction more clearly through soaking? Explain what that's like.

3. Are you ready for God to begin to pour out His creativity to you? Start opening your mind and heart to His creativity. Write what He's giving you.

4. What are some specific steps you can take to learn; the work of rest?

5. Describe in your own words what your Kingdom identity is or looks like.

Activation

As you soak this time, ask the Holy Spirit to stir up creativity within you. Like David, inquire of the Lord about specific things concerning your Kingdom assignment. You may want to use a pen and sheets of paper and write down downloads of ideas, plans, strategies and dreams you are getting in your spirit as you soak in His Presence.

Gleanings in His Presence

_____
_____
_____
_____
_____
_____
_____
_____
_____
_____
_____
_____
_____
_____
_____
_____

CHAPTER 9

Creating a Culture of Soaking

There are blessings that we experience as we come to Him individually. But there are other measures of grace that's available only when we come to Him as a family, as a Body.

The Kingdom of God is a supernatural kingdom and everything in it emanates from the very Nature of the King. Isaiah 9:7 says, *"There will be no end to the increase of His government or of peace, on the throne of David and over his kingdom, to establish it and to uphold it with justice and righteousness from then on and forevermore. The zeal of the LORD of hosts will accomplish this."* God's rule is ever increasing. God is so intentional in making sure His rule and reign transcend all spheres, realms, and ages for all eternity.

Since the beginning, it is God's desire to have a big family of mankind who will host His presence and will be His dwelling place here on earth. He mandated Adam and Eve to rule the earth and expand the borders of Eden. They were to establish the culture of heaven on earth and give rise to a people who will be naturally supernatural.

We understand that despite the temporary setback caused by the fall of man, God is so committed to accomplishing His purposes for all eternity. Jesus came to restore everything back to God's original intent and purpose in Creation. He came to establish the culture of heaven here on earth once again. Everything He did and taught, revealed God as Our Father and that His Kingdom is superior to all. He demonstrated that the Kingdom of God comes to invade the hearts of people and then through them it expands to the world around bringing transformation, where the realm of heaven comes down to earth.

God desires for His people to establish and cultivate the supernatural culture of heaven here on earth that will be sustained from generation to generation.

Merriam-Webster defines culture as the integrated pattern of human knowledge, belief, and behavior that depends upon the capacity for learning and transmitting knowledge to succeeding generations. God desires for His people to establish and cultivate the supernatural culture of heaven here on earth and sustain it from generation to generation.

Event to Movement

Cultures are shaped and established when people move from just having events, into creating lifestyles in the context of relationship. It doesn't happen overnight, it is a process. The supernatural Kingdom culture is sustained through the belief system we value and share. High value for God's manifest presence and intimacy with Him naturally bring us to deeper encounters with Him individually and corporately. In turn, we are exposed to the realm of the supernatural, the realm of heaven. Encounters with God bring profound transformation in and through us. To the degree His presence influences us, we will be able to influence the very world we live in effecting transformation, making it look just like heaven.

Kingdom culture is cultivated and enhanced through corporate experiences and shared revelations, testimonies of victories and exploits. These stories release the prophetic atmosphere and increase faith in the hearts of the people. Expectancy is elevated, shaping a corporate mindset that facilitates greater invasion and expressions of God's supernatural world on earth. As a result, the supernatural becomes the norm and the impossible becomes possible.

A single event will never have a long-term impact and sustainability until there's a culture formed and shaped that will continually steward and cultivate it. The great outpouring of the Holy Spirit in the Upper Room upon 120 disciples on the day of Pentecost gives us a clear illustration of this. From one event to one unstoppable movement, the Holy Spirit spreading across cultures transforming lives, cities, and nations as the Kingdom of God invaded hearts. This Kingdom event, forever etched in history, was sustained when the early believers devoted themselves continuously to lifestyles of prayer, fellowship, study of the apostles' doctrines, generosity, sacrifice, respect and honor, covenant, radical faith, boldness in proclamation and demonstration of the authority and power of the resurrected Jesus Christ. From that one event, a community influenced by the Holy Spirit was established. That community carried common core values that sustained a culture, and that culture changed cities and nations turning the world upside-down. Kingdom culture is the unstoppable force that will shape the cultures of this world.

Paul Yadao's Personal Journey

Creating the culture of soaking in the presence of God started with my own personal quest for deeper encounters with God. It started from one major event that brought a radical transformation within me. That event triggered an inner hunger for more of Him and His supernatural world.

May 2006 marked a major turning point in my life. Together, with my lovely wife Ahlmira, we had the privilege of attending Randy Clark's School of Healing at the Hosanna Lutheran Church in Lakeville, Minnesota. It was there we received a powerful impartation of the Father's Blessing that radically transformed our lives. We did not plan to attend the event; instead we came to participate in a mission consultation a week earlier. However, God had a different idea. He made a way for us to be there where He wanted us to be.

During one of the sessions of the conference, Leif Hetland preached a powerful message that God used to spark something within us. The message was about the Father's Love and Healing the Orphan Spirit. Leif shared his testimony of his encounter with the revelation of the Father's Love and how it radically transformed his life. At one point he mention there are orphan ministries and orphan ministers who were out there in the field trying to please God much like the older brother in the parable of the Prodigal Son. I felt

It was such a powerful moment to come into a revelation that God indeed is our Father Who loves us unconditionally and completely.

in my spirit that I've been an orphan minister myself. I then asked God to heal my heart and renew my mind. In that moment, I felt the love of the Father came upon me. Finally, I came to a life-changing revelation that He is indeed a Father unto me and I am His beloved son through Jesus. I experienced so much freedom within. I suddenly I realized the futility of my strivings, of trying to work for God and for the inheritance that He has made available to me through Jesus.

Leif released the Father's Blessing to everyone much like the declaration of the Father to His Beloved Son Jesus "This is My Beloved Son in Whom I am well-pleased". Those words resonated to the core of our beings, rearranging and uprooting things within which had been brought about by an orphan mindset. It was such a powerful moment, to step into a revelation that God indeed is our Father who loves us unconditionally and completely.

We asked Leif to be our spiritual father. By God's favor, he accepted us into his spiritual family. This was a tremendous blessing for us. We felt we finally came out of the orphanage that very moment and received immeasurable inheritance from our spiritual father.

After that, we went back to the Philippines radically transformed. From that moment, we saw fruit coming forth... tremendous blessings, anointing and favor flowing in and through us, such that we had never experienced in our lives before that moment.

The Fruit of Favor

Since that encounter in May 2006, God has literally poured upon us countless blessings in all aspects of our lives: family, ministry, finances, health, influence, anointing and ministry. We have experienced the tangible fruits of favor. The doors of opportunity swung wide open, and the needed resources followed. From just one nation, Malaysia, prior to receiving the Father's blessing, we opened up church planting works in Singapore, Cambodia, and Dubai. We have had opportunities to minister in other nations like Africa, India, and Pakistan through the ministry of Leif Hetland and Global Mission Awareness, as well as through our partnership with Hosanna Lutheran Church. We have seen major expansion in our movement especially in the area of church planting locally and internationally. We have seen God moved powerfully in our midst with mighty signs, wonders, and healings. Along with the major breakthroughs in the ministry, we have been experiencing tremendous material blessings. The supernatural has become so natural.

We released the impartation to our spiritual sons and daughters, as well as the rest of the Destiny family. We have witnessed the increase of favor and blessings in the lives of our people. There has been so much abundance, holistically in the lives of our people. In businesses, families, relationships, and ministries we have seen God's goodness flow from one person to another. Many came to know the Lord because of the goodness they have experienced in their lives as the Destiny people have gone out releasing and praying blessings over multitudes of people. The blessings have come in health, radical healings, supernatural provisions, employments, increases in income, restoration of relationships and much more.

Embraced by Love

To me the greatest blessing I received in May 2006 was the revelation and the genuine encounter of the Father's Love which has continuously and progressively embraced me. Finally I was out of the orphanage. I am now in my Father's house. I have been brought back to Eden, the place of His delight and affection. The Father's unconditional and perfect love to me was the very power that brought me deeper and deeper into His presence. I was so hungry for His love, His voice and His face. I know that He will be there every time I set my heart and my affection towards Him. I feel so much freedom and great measures of His glory come to me each time I am with my Father.

Prior to this encounter of the Father's love, I tried my best to wait upon the Lord in silence for at least an hour. Many times I did it out of discipline and striving. I had experienced levels of breakthroughs in my personal life and ministry, but it was hard to live up to, and try to please God with a mindset of an orphan. However with the revelation of the Father's love, and that in Christ I am now completely loved and accepted, my motivation shifted from striving to perform, to delighting in Him because I know He delights in me.

I have been a prisoner in the arms of my Father God who loves me as He loves Jesus the Beloved Son.

An hour of prayer is no longer enough to be in His presence. In fact, it's no longer how long I stay or pray, but it is now how deep the Holy Spirit brings me into His presence. I have been a prisoner in the arms of my Father God who loves me as He loves Jesus, the beloved son. I so love it! There are no more walls, no more condemnation, no more striving. There's only love, only delight, only goodness.

I share my testimonies, the fresh downloads of revelations I received and the supernatural encounters I have with God in my personal soaking time. His presence validates what I share on a personal level, or in a corporate setting. Healings, signs and wonders increased tremendously in my life. These things come out as the fruit of my deep encounters with God. Those who have heard my stories caught the heart to soak in the presence of God.

By His grace, my personal journey became a corporate inspiration to many to experience God deeply in soaking prayer. Because of this, several individuals joined me in my soaking times in the middle of the night from 11pm to 3am. More and more came to join me until such a time when we established a corporate soaking time every Thursday night in our ministry center. From that time on corporate soaking spread to the different churches of Destiny and it became part of the culture of our spiritual family.

Since then, we are seeing miracles, signs, and wonders happening in different settings and contexts. There were countless testimonies that people attributed to their personal encounters with God during their time of soaking. The Kingdom of God invades lives transforming marriages, healing broken bodies, releasing dreams, breaking bondages, supplying supernatural provisions, blessings and favors, creativity, salvations and breakthroughs. Even our biological children, Dave and Sophie know how to soak in the presence of God and they love it. The supernatural things become so natural to them; it has become the norm. At their young age, they recognize the manifest presence of God and intimacy with Him is what shapes their lives.

One is Many

The leadership of Moses and David is a great inspiration to me. Their lives have modeled to us that in the Kingdom of God one is many. Their personal encounters with God and the levels of intimacy with Him became the inspiration, the catalyst, and the standard for their people and the generations that followed. They desired not just to grow in their personal relationship with Jehovah God, but they paved the way for others to come into levels of encounters with Him. Their personal dealings with God shaped their leadership, and they brought others with them in the Presence of God.

In Exodus 24, the Lord told Moses to go up to the mountain with the priests, Aaron, Nadab and Abihu, and the seventy elders of Israel and worship Him. In verse 10 it says, *"and they saw the God of Israel; and under His feet there appeared to be a pavement of sapphire, as clear as the sky itself. Yet He did not stretch out His hand against the nobles of the sons of Israel; and they saw God, and they ate and drank."* The elders and the priests had an encounter with Jehovah God because of the place of favor Moses had as a friend of God. His personal history with God became the platform for others to experience God.

We are called to bring others into the presence of God. God desires to fill His temple with His presence. The more we bring living stones into His Presence, the more of Him we experience. There are blessings we experience as we come to Him individually. But there are other measures of grace available only when we come to Him as a family, as a Body.

Some Practical Tips in Leading a Corporate Soaking Session

Preparation

There must be a place conducive and comfortable enough for soaking. We advise that enough space should be available for people to lie down or sit comfortably without crowding. Be sure there's proper ventilation in the room, good soft lighting and sound and a setting that would give people freedom to pour out their emotions to God without disturbing others.

As a leader, it is important that we come to the soaking meeting prepared. This means practically and spiritually. Ask the Holy Spirit for inspiration and guidance to the flow of the soaking meeting. You can prepare the songs you would be using ahead of time. The last thing you would want to happen in your corporate soaking is to be so disorganized to the point of cutting the flow of the Holy Spirit in your midst. Arrange the songs in such a way that people are inspired to go deeper into the Presence of God. There are songs that will be so crucial in setting the tone and the depths of the soaking, be sensitive to this.

Exhortation

It's important to give a brief overview and explanation to people what the meeting is all about and what to expect in the meeting. You can also give some practical tips how they would go about it. The people in your group have to understand the importance of what you are about to do. This is especially essential to the first timers. The clearer you are able to communicate this, the better.

Facilitation

For the first part of soaking join the whole group and allow the Holy Spirit to flow through you, stirring up emotions of compassion and love. Stay for a period of time and allow Him to fill you within and sense His leading. As a leader, ask the Holy Spirit how you would be able to facilitate others into personal encounters with Him. Approach individuals that He's leading you to minister to. Softly release the words, or impressions that you are receiving in behalf of that person.

Sometimes, you'll sense a prayer rise within you. Utter it on behalf of the other person, and see them respond and eventually get into the flow of His Presence. Sometimes it could be a prophetic word or a promise you have to release to facilitate awakening of faith and hunger in that person's heart. You could ask other mature believers in the group to help in facilitating others towards encountering God.

At this point, you can also give a corporate word of inspiration to encourage them to focus and to go deeper. Sometimes I would inspire people to write down what they have been receiving in the presence of God, ideas, words, prophecies, pictures, or deep emotions.

Adoration

You may want to inspire the group to express their longings to Him and let the Holy Spirit take control over their desires. It is powerful when individuals express their hearts for the Lord, but it is equally important to have a corporate expression of our passions and desire for God's presence.

Declaration

During our corporate soaking we usually lead people into a time of declaration. This aspect is necessary. Remember the Royal Priesthood ministry? We usually devote the last fifteen minutes of our corporate soaking to making decrees and declarations. As we are soaked in the presence of God, the Holy Spirit gives us prayers to pray and to declare over circumstances and situations, and over each other.

Sharing

This is the last part of the corporate soaking. Encourage people to share their journey into the depths of God and allow for prophetic words to be given. If there are specific prayer needs raised up, or prophetic words that would be encouraging to the people, this is the best time to share it. Always end with a word of prayer and encourage others to look forward to the next soaking session.

Questions for Personal Ponder or Group Discussion

1. Do you have a corporate body or relationship to begin cultivating this culture of soaking? Who or whom?

2. Have you struggled with an orphan way of thinking? In what ways and areas?

3. Can you feel the embrace of the Father's love? Just allow His arms to wrap around you, be still and bask in His love and presence as a son/daughter.

4. How will you use your experiences while soaking to affect and bless others?

5. What specific part of Paul's personal journey spoke to you the most and why?

Activation

It is important that you are able to share your personal journey with God to others. This may awaken hunger and desire for them to go deep into the Presence of God. Although, not all of the things you experience in the secret place with God are to be shared right away, for some of them could be for the future, it is important that you have people around you who would share your journey into the Presence of God. And many times the Lord confirms His Word through several individuals having similar experiences with you.

Gleanings in His Presence

_____
_____
_____
_____
_____
_____
_____
_____
_____
_____
_____
_____
_____
_____

APPENDICES

APPENDIX I

Dictionary Definitions

SOAK - to become thoroughly wet, or saturated by immersion, to drink excessively, to become drunk to take in, to soak up.

LIE DOWN - to place oneself or be in a prostrate position in order to rest. To accept without protest or opposition.

QUIET - to be untroubled, free from activities, distractions, still, calm.

REST - to relax from exertion, or labor, repose, sleep, a pause or interval.

LISTEN - to concentrate on hearing something, take heed, pay attention.

WAIT - to stay in one place, or remain inactive in expectation of something.

APPENDIX II

It's all in the Plan

> *"Drink, yes, drink deeply, O beloved ones!*
> Song of Solomon 5:1

In the beginning God created man and woman. His greatest joy was the close fellowship (or communion) He had with them as they walked and talked together in the garden, enjoying the cool of the day. But it didn't last.

Satan brought sin into the world and broke that precious, intimate relationship. So man began to search for something to fill the emptiness in his heart.

Thank God that Jesus came and restored mankind into relationship with the Father.

Now the Holy Spirit comes to soften our hearts, re-kindle our love for our heavenly Dad and make us ready for a new love relationship. This time is as the Bride of Christ, with Jesus as our husband.

The marriage fest of Jesus is coming closer!

This is what these sessions are all about: Us being cleansed, prepared and anointed, just as Queen Esther did before her meeting with the King (she prepared herself by soaking in precious bath oils for a period of six months before her meeting with the King of Persia. The favor she gained meant the salvation of the nation of Israel). It's simply us coming to be with our Father, no shopping lists, no agendas, just ourselves being still in His arms of love.

So come and settle down, relax and enjoy a good long soak.

What do you mean "Soaking"?
The old word would be "wait on the Lord" or "tarry", but there is an emphasis on rest, as over against striving in prayer. Soft intimate worship music will help you quiet your soul and draw you near to God.

Why would I want to soak?
There is a deep need in every one of us to be close to God. Some have described it as a "God-shaped" vacuum inside of every human heart that longs to be fulfilled.

How do I know I need to soak?
If you are spiritually dry, soaking can revitalize your spirit.
If you long to move more powerfully in the gifts of the Spirit, soaking can help you hear God clearly.
If you are looking for fresh vision and direction in life, soaking can bring it.
If you are hurting inside, soaking can ease the pain.
If you are about to start something new and need the Lord's strengthening, soaking can refresh you.
If you are searching for an answer to some problem/situation, soaking can help
you find the way.
If you carry responsibilities, soaking can lift your burden. If you are trapped by habitual sin, soaking can empower you to break free.
If you are having relational difficulties, soaking can give you new resources of grace, patience and love.
If you simply want to have more intimacy in your love for your heavenly Father, soaking can take you deeper.

So do I just lie down with a blank mind?
No! Lie down with your mind and heart set on Jesus. Give all your worries and cares to the Lord. Talk to Him about them.

Pray a prayer that says to God something like, "I invite You to come and search my heart. Come close and let me know Your love." Let worship rise up inside you and give yourself to the Lord. If you become distracted then refocus on Jesus. Remind yourself why you are soaking and listen to the worship.

Can I trust it is the Holy Spirit working?
These sessions are covered in prayer to create a safe place. Give the Holy Spirit permission to work in your heart, don't try to analyze things. The Lord has no favorites; He will always give the Holy Spirit to those who ask: "If a son asks for bread from any father among you, will he give him a stone? Or if he asks for a fish, will he give him a serpent instead of a fish? Or if he asks for an egg, will he offer him a scorpion? If you then, being evil know how to give good gifts to your children, how much more shall your heavenly Father give the Holy Spirit to them that ask Him? (Luke 11:11-13)

Other spirits can't come near us when the Holy Spirit is around—expect His divine protection.

How long do I stay down for?
It takes most people at least ten minutes before they stop thinking about the day's events or future plans and come to a place of rest. So it's unlikely you would get much out of soaking if you do it for less than fifteen minutes.

We have found that the Holy Spirit comes in waves. As you wait, another wave will come to take you deeper into the presence of the Lord. So, the longer you soak the
better!

Once I get up can I come back for more?
Yes, it is often good to get up, have a break and pray over things the Lord has shown you (either on your own or with another), write things down so you won't forget, then return and soak some more. Just be sensitive to others about you and move quietly.

How will I know when God is finished?
The more you soak the easier it will become to recognize when to stop. Often you will sense a lifting of the anointing and a reviving

of energy. Remember, you will never get beyond the need for more of the Holy Spirit.

Do I have to lie down?
No, you can soak sitting in a chair if you find it more comfortable. Being still and at rest is the key. It aligns our bodies with our hearts' attitude of submissiveness and attentiveness to God. Lying down helps to minimize the distractions caused by activity in the room.

How will I know if soaking is doing me any good?
Many people feel immediate benefits such as a renewed love for the Lord, a lifting of weights or fresh energy. Often evidence of long term changes is discovered later when back in daily life.

What if I fall asleep?
That's perfectly valid. Deep, Holy Spirit sleep is very good for us, especially in difficult and stressful times. (Gen. 2:21, 15:12; Dan. 10:8-10; Luke 9:32)